How to Succeed in
NETWORK
MARKETING

How to Succeed in
NETWORK
MARKETING

LEONARD S. HAWKINS

PIATKUS

Copyright © 1991 Leonard S. Hawkins

First published in 1991 by
Judy Piatkus (Publishers) Ltd
5 Windmill Street, London W1P 1HF

*The author asserts his moral rights to be
identified as author of this work*

British Library Cataloguing in Publication Data
Hawkins, Leonard
    How to succeed in network marketing.
    I. Title
    658.8

    ISBN 0 – 7499 – 1057 – 7

Edited by Carol Franklin

Set in 11/13pt Compugraphic Times by
Action Typesetting Ltd, Gloucester
Printed and bound in Great Britain by
Bookcraft Ltd, Midsomer Norton, Avon

To
Robert D'Aubingy
You taught me how to live again
Thank you

ACKNOWLEDGEMENTS

MANY people have contributed towards the creation of this book. Rarely is anything in life is accomplished solely by one person: most undertakings are a team effort. That was certainly the case of *How to Succeed in Network Marketing*.

I would like to express my gratitude to all those who freely shared their insights into the business. Without their input this book would have been considerably the poorer. Unfortunately, the constraints of space would not allow me to relate all their stories.

In addition I would like to say a special thank you to the following:

Richard Berry, director of the Direct Selling Association;

Tom Davies, sales director of Kleneze Homecare Ltd;

John Doughty, general manager of Nature's Sunshine Products Inc.;

Martin Williams, sales and marketing manager of Amway UK Ltd;

Mike Lewis;

Gill Cormode and Judy Piatkus of Piatkus Books for their dedication to helping me produce 'the best possible book'.

And last, but by no means least, I would like to thank my wife, Irene, for her tireless support — and simply for being Irene.

CONTENTS

PREFACE

IN the early days of any enterprise it is of great benefit to have as much information at one's fingertips as possible. To have access to the wisdom of those who have gone before is a boon of incalculable value.

Nearly all the books available on the subject of network marketing up to now have been geared for the US market. Many of these are fine books, but the UK is not the USA and I felt that there was a need for a work written with an understanding of the UK market. I also believed that UK networkers would be interested to read the success stories of people who have made it on this side of the Atlantic.

How To Succeed in Network Marketing is designed to enable you to do just that — to succeed, by whatever standards you choose to measure that success. By putting its principles to work in your life you can come to realise those dreams which otherwise would have remained only dreams.

INTRODUCTION

THE concept of network or multi-level marketing (MLM) is much maligned and misunderstood. It is a multi-million pound operation that is one of the fastest growing businesses in the world. The principles of networking are even taught at the prestigious Harvard Business School. Around 20 per cent of the estimated 500,000 millionaires in the USA have made their money through network marketing — and the signs are that the UK is set to go the same way.

Thousands of people across the UK are already joining in this gold-rush, developing part-time incomes of over £10,000 per year; full-time incomes of £20,000 – £50,000; and, for the few, blue chip incomes exceeding £10,000 per **MONTH**! These successful people come from all walks of life. Some were on the verge of bankruptcy before they came to the business, others were already millionaires. Teachers, salespeople, decorators, doctors, engineers, airline pilots — the list of previous occupations scans the spectrum of human endeavour. The qualities they all possess in common are commitment, the ability to persevere and a willingness to learn.

This is not a 'rah-rah, go-for-it' type of book, but a practical, working manual which will benefit you for many years as your business continues to grow. The principles of network marketing may be simple, but putting them into practice is not always so easy unless you have foreknowledge of the pitfalls.

In the course of extensive research for this book I have talked to hundreds of successful people at all levels within the industry, from managing directors of multinational companies to housewives earning pin money. This book is a distillation of knowledge gained from actual experience and proven over time to be successful.

Whether you wish to earn £100,000 a year or just an extra £30 –

£50 a week, there is something within these pages for you. The techniques for the successful building and continued operation of a network marketing business have worked for thousands. If you adopt an open, enquiring, *teachable* mind, those same techniques could soon be bringing *you* success and prosperity!

PART ONE

UNDERSTANDING NETWORK MARKETING

1. NETWORK MARKETING AND YOU

WOULD you like to be financially independent, free to arrange your own schedule for the day and be able to take the day off without having to fear the consequences? Would you like to be able to go on those sumptuous holidays which beckon enticingly from the windows of every high street travel agent? Perhaps your desire is for that new car in the showroom which you walk past every day on the way to work; a house like the one you and your wife have admired fleetingly as you drove to the supermarket; or to be able to retire early on a comfortable pension? Or maybe your desires are simpler — more involvement with you family, the time to play with your children, or to create that sculpture, painting or novel you have promised yourself you would get around to for so long? I'm sure you could add several goals of your own to that list.

It is little wonder then that so many people are unhappy holding down jobs which force them into strait-jackets of conformity, with bosses who care little or nothing for their well-being and happiness, but only for the profit and loss accounts at the end of the year. Even many of those who own their own businesses are tied hand and foot to the demands of employees, unions and landlords.

What would you do if a proposition was presented to you which promised to grant you most if not all of these desires? A proposition that promised real freedom from wage slavery, totally flexible working hours and an amount of money few dare even to dream of earning. My guess is that, once you saw it was genuine and that you had the talent to make it work, you would go for it like a greyhound after a hare.

Multi level marketing (MLM) can offer you *all* of the above.

'Oh yes', I can hear you saying, 'I've heard this all before. It's just another quack get-rich-quick scheme for people with more greed in their heads than brains.'

I know just how you feel, because I felt that way too before I discovered how much real money people were making in this business and how much leisure and freedom of choice they had in their lives. That was when I decided to take a serious look at a business which turns over several *billion* pounds each year worldwide, and it is a most fascinating world.

Network marketing is *not* pyramid selling

'It's pyramid selling, that's what it is', says the bar room expert, holding forth in his local while he downs another pint. 'You won't see me taken in by that nonsense. I'm no fool.' And with that he proceeds to spend the rest of the evening bemoaning his life, his mortgage, etc ... Well, you've heard it all before, haven't you?

We should dispose of the pyramid selling slur at the outset as it's an objection which is frequently raised. When you start your business you will come across similar objections, but you will be able easily and naturally to apply the techniques learned within these pages to overcome them.

Let us assume that you are face to face with your bar room expert and are given the chance to explain network marketing when he says 'It sounds like pyramid selling to me.'

You reply by saying, 'I understand why you might think that. I was worried about it at first. But then I realised the difference between network marketing and the old pyramid con. Tell me, what do you understand pyramid selling to be?'

Your bar room expert will probably admit at this stage that really he doesn't know much about pyramid selling at all, apart from the fact that it was a con. You will find that most people, when confronted by someone who demands that they clarify their statements on this issue can't do it.

You go on to explain: During the 1960s and 1970s several rogue companies caused a great deal of grief to many people by exploiting their desire to better their lives. Collins dictionary has this to say about it: 'A practice adopted by some manufacturers of advertising for distributors and selling them batches of goods. The first distributors then advertise for more distributors who are sold subdivisions of the original batch at an increased price. This process continues until the final distributors are left with a stock that is unsaleable except at a loss.'

Many people were the victims of a practice known as 'garage filling'. That was all they did, they filled their garages with useless product they had bought for several thousand pounds. That was the only place their product ever went. It never actually got to a retail consumer as it was impossible to sell. The pyramid companies also paid a recruitment fee simply for introducing someone to the company.

Network marketing, on the other hand, does not require a heavy investment. In fact the law states that no one may invest more than an initial £75 in their business for the first seven days. In networking the emphasis is on getting the goods to an end consumer. Unless product is sold to a consumer no one is going to make any money. There is nothing to be made in merely signing someone into the business; you have to make sales in order to receive any money. Also, the wholesale price of the product does not increase if you simply pass it on to someone else. Hence you make no money directly out of the people you bring into the business (although your company will pay bonuses proportionate to the volume of business your group does each month). As a final nail in the coffin of the pyramid selling myth, there is a clause in all MLM contracts which states that the parent company will buy back any unsold product if their distributors are unable to dispose of it.

By this time your bar room expert is probably feeling a little foolish for making any comparison with pyramiding in the first place with so little actual knowledge at his disposal, and you will have persuaded him of the legitimacy of the business. You could also add that pyramid selling is illegal (*see* Appendix B); that if you analyse the corporate structure of any large firm you will see a pyramid shape emerging (from a single chairman at the top to half a dozen vice-chairmen, to numerous managers and sub-managers, to the vast number of people who work on the shop floor); and that the largest multi-level company in the world, Amway, has been trading for over thirty years and generates retail sales of nearly US $2 billion! How could an unworkable con continue for so long and make that sort of money?

The cynics who stand on the sidelines of life can easily be thwarted when faced with the facts.

So what *is* network marketing?

Networking is a system of distributing goods and services to retail consumers. During the 1990s the concept will be applied to an ever increasing range of products.

It is a friends-doing-business-with-friends method of retailing. Let's say you decide to come into the business. By yourself you can reach only so many people during the course of your day, week or month. You earnings are therefore limited. The only way in which you can increase your income is to open another outlet for your goods or service. In a conventional business that would mean taking on staff and opening another shop, with all the hassles and high overheads that would entail.

Life is much simpler in the world of network marketing. Let's assume that your friend Judy has also decided to come into the business. You sign her up into the company using a form which will be supplied. She then becomes your *downline*. At this juncture I should point out that those whom you bring into your business become your downlines, and those who brought you into the business are termed your *uplines*. You teach Judy how to retail the products, and, by adding her sales to yours, you have immediately increased your turnover.

But it doesn't stop there, for Judy will bring other people into her business (i.e. *sponsor* them) who will buy and sell products and then sponsor people themselves. So by bringing Judy into your business, and teaching her correctly, you will eventually multiply your turnover several times over.

'But surely I will not make as much money from Judy's sales?' you may ask, 'After all, she has to make her own profit. I think I'd be better off going out and doing all the selling myself and taking a larger percentage.'

Well, that is correct – up to a point. Consider this analogy. Bert is to set up a window cleaning business. If he works hard he will probably make about £200 a week. But he can't earn any more than this. For the rest of his life Bert will be doing nothing more than earning a living.

Now, supposing he were to advertise for thirty others to come and help him. He trains those people to work as efficiently as he, so that they are soon earning £200 a week also. If, as a reward for his efforts, he takes only 5 per cent of each person's turnover he will have an income of £300. Add that to his personal £200 and Bert is now on £500 a week — a much healthier income you must agree. Essentially that is the essence of network marketing — a group of independent businesses working together for their mutual benefit.

SUCCESS CHECK

Network marketing is:

★ a system of distributing goods and services

★ a friends-doing-business-with friends method of retailing

★ a group of independent businesses working together for their mutual benefit

---

The advantages of network marketing

It is important to recognise that, although network marketing is a method of selling direct to the general public, it should not be confused with the direct selling of double glazing, encyclopedias, etc (although the top networking firms are, paradoxically, members of the Direct Selling Association — the DSA). A significant difference between multi-level and conventional direct sales is that most direct sales people are simply salespersons working for a parent company. They are invariably self-employed, but still have to answer to the whip of their managers like a waged employee. They have no security and are liable to lose their jobs if they take too many holidays or upset the boss.

In contrast, the distributors involved in network marketing would shy away from the idea of becoming hard-nosed, high-pressure salespeople. Multi-level products are invariably soft-sell lines which makes it easy for a wide cross-section of people to become involved. One of the appeals of the business is the level of personal contact and service which has all but disappeared in many of our impersonal high street shops. This, together with the convenience of having the goods delivered straight to the customer's home, makes network marketing an attractive proposition for both customer and distributor.

Also, all network businesses are independent and as such determine their own sales targets and working hours. You can earn as much, or as little, as you like. If you want to go on holiday for three months you can do so secure in the knowledge that your business will still be there when you return.

Overheads are minimal. Most distributors work from home, eliminating the need for expensive office and showroom space. They buy product direct from the manufacturer and sell direct to the customer. There are no other middlemen or wholesalers to take a cut of the profit. And there is little or no advertising, apart from advertisements to recruit other associates to the business.

Networking has been likened to franchising without the franchise fee. There is some truth in the comparison. You are in business for yourself, but not by yourself. You have the ongoing support of your upline and the parent company, and all the problems you are likely to meet will have already been solved by someone else.

When you consider that the rewards can equal, or even better, the most successful franchises, the financial investment in networking is incrediby small. Unlike most conventional retailing businesses there is no need to buy thousands of pounds worth of stock.

SUCCESS CHECK

The advantages of network marketing:

★ personal contact and service for your customer

★ delivery of goods to your customer's home

★ network businesses are independent and determine their own sales targets and working hours

★ can be run from home

★ minimal overheads

★ maximum legal start-up cost is only £75

★ you do not need to invest in large amounts of stock

★ you are in business for yourself, but not by yourself

The investment you need to make in order to succeed

Although your financial investment may be low, you will need to invest more than money in your network marketing business if you are going to be successful.

When you are first considering setting up a network marketing business, you need to consider the whole range of your commitment to that business. If you plant nothing you should not expect to harvest a bumper crop.

Think about the following points. Understanding them will help you decide if this business is for you − applying them will enable you to succeed.

Investment in product

A certain amount of stock is needed even for the most basic multi-level business. You must use the products yourself (how can you expect others to buy if you do not believe in your goods enough to use them yourself?), and you need to have a selection of products to show retail customers and potential business associates.

Teachability

This is one of the most important assets you can bring to this business. Networking is unlike any other line of work. It is about a lot of people each selling a small amount of product. People whose minds have been so conditioned by other work practices that they cannot change will inevitably fail.

Many people come to network marketing after having successfully built a conventional business from scratch. They can be so used to doing everything themselves that it can take a long time for them to realise that they have uplines whose help and advice they can draw on at any time. If such people do not learn to tap into the experience of others the business can be hard going. But, once they realise the sheer waste of effort involved in constantly reinventing the wheel, their business will begin to take off.

A good multi-level company will have training laid on for you to participate in. Make full use of it. Ask questions, find out as much about your company, product and the marketing plan as you can. Learn well, for soon you will be responsible for teaching others.

10

Sharing knowledge with others

Unlike the cut-throat competitiveness of the traditional business world, in network marketing there is no hugging of secrets close to your chest. It is just the opposite in fact – the more you share your experience with your downlines the more successful their businesses, and hence yours, will become. Your commitment to your downlines is to help them succeed and your income will grow in direct proportion to their success.

The heart of networking is helping and teaching people. You help your retail customers by supplying them with a product which they need. And you help your downlines by teaching them how to achieve the realisation of their dreams. As well as the financial rewards you achieve you will find it a great joy to help other people pay off their debts, buy a larger home, or send their children to the best schools.

Shouldering responsibility

When you start your business you will become an independent distributor for a manufacturing company. The key word in that sentence is independent. You will have access to help and support from your uplines and from your parent company. But they will not build your business for you. You are the person who will ultimately be responsible for the success or failure of your business.

You will undoubtedly come across problems, especially in the early days of your business, and how you handle these problems will have considerable bearing on the size to which your business will ultimately grow.

The attitude you need to adopt is that of viewing responsibility and problems as interesting challenges – challenges you can easily shoulder and overcome.

Committing time to your business

Not only must you give time each week to your business but you must give your business time to grow. A part-time commitment could be as little as five to ten hours a week, while full-time commitment could mean as many as one hundred hours a week. The choice is yours. Obviously the more time you spend on your business the faster your income will climb.

You will find that some people expect overnight riches. These are the people who say, 'I'll give it a try for a couple of months, but if I'm not on £10,000 a month at the end of that time, then I quit.'

Say to these people, 'But how long have you been working at your old job?'

'Ten years, or so', they reply.

'So after ten years you still aren't earning £10,000 a month?'

'Of course not.'

'So you expect your MLM business to achieve in two months what you have failed to achieve over the last ten years?'

'Well ...'.

Give your business a year's trial. You have a lot to learn and you are bound to make a few mistakes. Note that many conventional businesses do not expect to show any profit *at all* for two or three years. You will not have to wait that long. But do remember to treat your business as a business.

Showing enthusiasm

How crucial that word *enthusiasm* is. It was deliberately kept until last for that very reason. If you forget everything else that is written in this book try at least to remember enthusiasm. You can do a retail demonstration and forget half the things you were going to say, but customers will still buy if you communicate your enthusiasm. You can present the business opportunity and leave out half the detail, but people will still join you if you are enthusiastic about what you are doing.

It is useful to be familiar with a few basic sales techniques. But no amount of clever talk will ever substitute for honest enthusiasm. In network marketing this is especially important as you are working with friends and colleagues. They do not expect slick sales patter, and may even be turned off buying because of it. They will, however, expect you to be enthusiastic about something which you believe in.

Imagine that you are at a barbecue. Across the lawn you hear the sizzle of hamburgers and onions on the charcoal grill. The mouth-watering aroma wafts into your nostrils. I'll bet you want to taste one of those burgers, don't you? How long will it be before you are queuing up for yours?

Notice that what you get excited about is not the burger, but the *sound* and *smell* of the meat and onions sizzling on the grill and all that it conjured up in your mind. A good barbecue salesman would be selling his customers on the idea of that sizzling aroma stimulating

12

everyone's taste-buds. The same is true in network marketing.

Your enthusiasm is the sizzle, with the product or business the burger. What your customers buy is not the bare facts of the product or business — but your sizzling, contagious enthusiasm!

SUCCESS CHECK

Your investment in network marketing:

★ you must be willing to invest in a small amount of stock

★ you must be willing to learn

★ you must be willing to share your knowledge

★ you must be willing to accept responsibility

★ you must be willing to give time to your business

★ you must be willing to show your enthusiasm

Network Marketing Success Story
ANDY AND VAL PRIVETT
London

Andy and Val ran an insurance brokerage business prior to coming into network marketing, but were forced out by new legislation which increased costs beyond their ability to absorb. They then tried their hand at an advertising franchise, but the parent company folded. Dismayed but not disheartened they continued to be open-minded and positive about the future.

Then, when an old school friend introduced them to Amway, Andy became very excited at the potential inherent in the business, although it was to take Val another two months to fully understand what they were doing.

Since they joined the company in 1981 Andy and Val have come to view Amway more as a way of life than as hard work. They say that, contrary to conventional business, network marketing is a team effort where everyone helps everyone else. All are striving for the same thing with no boss to knock them if they step out of line. They love the freedom to schedule their lives the way *they* want.

During the early days of their business they made the mistake of getting over excited when trying to sponsor others. They noticed a difference between enthusiasm and raw excitement. And they realised that over-zealous excitement, especially in the UK, can repel rather than attract people. Similarly, when they sponsor today they talk only in generalities, so that their prospect's brain does not become overloaded and switch off. They advise not to give too much information too soon.

In conventional employment Andy found that the people above you on the promotional scale can often hinder your own promotion. They can make life difficult for others simply to protect themselves, seeing up-and-coming staff as a potential threat to their own jobs. He found that the better he performed, the higher his targets became, areas were altered to make his task harder, and he experienced an ongoing battle with his management.

Not so in Amway. With network marketing he has found that his uplines actively encourage him and Val to be as successful as possible. He has found that, in this business, everyone wins.

2. How to choose your Company

AT this point it is important we introduce the vehicle for your success: the company and its product range. Your choice of parent company can mean the difference between success and failure in this business. It is important to choose the most appropriate one for you. This chapter will give you several criteria so that you can make an informed decision.

Types of product

The products you may be offered to sell fall broadly into two categories: consumable products and speciality products.

Consumable products

Goods such as vitamins, household cleaning supplies, cosmetics, etc, in fact anything which is used up and repeats regularly comes into this category. Individually, this type of product will not justify a lot of time spent retailing. The profit on each sale simply is not high enough. But, if you want your involvement in selling products to be minimal, this is the type of product you should be looking at. All you need is for ten to twenty of your friends or colleagues to purchase a small quantity each month. Obviously there can be nothing approaching the hard sell involved here.

One approach with this type of product is to present *everyone* you prospect with your business plan. This way, those who come in will at least be wholesale users, and will have the potential of being trained to bring other people into the business. Of course, if they don't want to commit themselves to anything at all, and prefer to pay retail prices, you can still sell them some product.

This approach has the advantage of creating a higher feeling of self-esteem in the person doing the presenting. It is all a question of attitude. Many people may find the selling of household cleansers not particularly gratifying to the ego. But if you see yourself as running your own business – and approach others in this light – you will *feel* professional, and your prospect will pick up on this.

Almost anyone can make a success of retailing this type of product. To make any substantial money, however, you will need to be bringing large numbers of people into your business. So how are you going to do that? Simply tell them? Possibly, although your success rate could be fairly low. Alternatively, you could *sell* the business plan to them. Maybe you do not like the sound of selling someone on a business. If so, take a look at Chapter 5, where you will come to understand exactly what is meant by the word 'selling'.

Speciality products

Speciality products are larger items such as water and air filtration equipment, water softeners, smoke detectors, etc.

A substantial turnover can be generated from the retail sales of speciality products. Therefore, relative to a consumable oriented business, you will not need to sponsor so many people in order to create the same total business volume. The drawback is that those you do sponsor will need to be far more sales oriented since because these products do not repeat frequently, there is the need to constantly find new customers. And there is no possibility of recruiting an army of 'users' as there is nothing being consumed which will create the need for repeat orders.

But we are still not in the hard sell business. Network marketing companies with speciality products usually use the free trial approach. The idea is that once the customer has got used to using the product for a week or so they will not want to lose it, and you have got a sale. It is much easier to offer your customer a week's free trial than it is to sell them something straight off. And from these retail demonstrations can come new recruits for your business. After all, who could be better than a satisfied customer to take your product into the market place?

Personal considerations

How much selling?

As we have been discussing, some products require more selling than others. One of the fundamental questions you should ask yourself is this: would you feel happier with a product with a high retail profit, but which needs a little bit of sales technique; or would you prefer to distribute a large range of goods, often in catalogue form, making less money on each individual sale but with the advantage of repeat orders?

The choice is yours, and yours alone. No one can make the decision for you. Neither is intrinsically better than the other and, at the end of the day, the incomes generated seem to be comparable.

Go along to the public meetings held by all the companies in which you are interested. You can find out who organises them locally by phoning the head office of the company. Talk to several people and ask questions of them. Try to gain an insight from their answers as to what running that format of business would be like, and whether it would suit your nature and requirements.

Your partner's support

When you experience difficulties with your business, and everyone does from time to time, you will find the support of your partner to be of incalculable value. Everyone needs a boost from time to time and your spouse will be ideally placed to give you yours.

You would do well to discuss your proposed business with your spouse before becoming actively involved. Ideally, you should take them along to a meeting so they can judge at first hand for themselves. Can they get enthusiastic about the company and/or product range? Whether or not you want to make network marketing work as a team business, and many do, is a question the two of you must address.

It is not essential that your partner becomes involved in your business, but do get their moral support. If you have problems in this regard let them see the benefits – take them out to dinner on your profits or buy them a surprise present, explaining that you can afford it because of the business. Most spouses will soon become warm to the idea of network marketing once they can see some results.

Unless you have the backing of your partner you will have an extremely difficult time making any sort of success with this business. Few people can take on the world and then come home to someone who bursts their bubble of enthusiasm.

Note: The above comments apply to those who already have close life partners. It is not meant to suggest that a partner is a prerequisite for success. Single people can do equally well.

A people business

Different products and companies attract different types of personalities. As this is predominately a people business, and you will be working closely with those who are in the business now, it is important that you feel at ease in their presence. The way to decide is simply to visit several meetings, mix freely, and get a feel of what is going on for yourself.

Enthusiasm

Unless you can raise a high level of enthusiasm for the products you are considering selling you are destined for failure. If you come up against this problem initially do not be deterred. There are many network marketing companies, and a lot of products to choose from. Shop around until you find a range with which you feel comfortable.

SUCCESS CHECK

Personal factors:

★ Would you feel most comfortable with consumable or speciality products?

★ Do you have the support of your spouse?

★ Do you feel empathy with those already in the business?

★ Can you get enthusiastic about the product range?

Analysing a potential company

Making the correct choice of a company to work with is vitally important. You can have all the enthusiasm in the world, but it will do you no good unless you direct it well. Your enthusiasm will soon wane if you sign up with a dud company. Below you will find listed the points to be aware of when analysing a prospective company.

The product range

1. Is there already a warm, receptive market for the product? Some people can sell sand to Bedouins and snow to Eskimos – but could you?

2. How large is your potential market? A product which appeals only to a very limited group of customers is not going to sell very well.

3. Will the products sell at the price you have to charge in order to make a profit? This is the delicate balance of the supply and demand curve. If you see evidence of strong retailing going on by the people already in the business, this will be a good indication that the company has done its sums correctly.

4. Can you make enough profit from selling the goods to justify the time expended? Only you can answer this and your answer will depend on the value you place on your time. For instance, if you can earn £15 an hour from your existing employment – but only £8 an hour from retailing – then you will obviously not feel inclined to sell much product. In this instance you would be better off spending most of your time sponsoring. On the other hand, if £8 an hour looks good in comparison to your present wage, you will be motivated to get out and get selling straight away.

5. Does the product repeat? This is important. If you have no repeat sales you will continually have to find new customers. This can be extremely tiring and you will also be unable to build up a retirement fund. The capacity of network marketing to provide you with a comfortable retirement depends on your establishing a network of businesses, who, in turn, supply a network of customers who reorder on a regular basis.

If you can see a huge profit to be made in the short term the lack of repeatability may not deter you. However, the vast majority of

19

successful people have made their money by distributing repeat products, thus producing a regenerative income.

6. Finally, what is the company's commitment to new product research and development? It is important for any growing company to be continually introducing new products as this increases the size of your market.

SUCCESS CHECK

The products:

★ Is there a market for the products?

★ How large and receptive is that market?

★ Are the products priced to sell?

★ Are the products priced for profit?

★ Do the products repeat?

★ Are new products introduced regularly?

The marketing plan

The structure of each network marketing company and their marketing plans may differ, but there are a few pointers to consider which apply across the board. One of the most important is that the plan must be easily understood and simply explained. As with every aspect of network marketing it must be possible for large numbers of people to comprehend it and explain it to others. If this is not the case you will soon run into problems.

Study the plan in depth. Although it is vital to be able to explain it to your prospects, it is also important to know where your own efforts should be concentrated for the greatest profitability. For instance, is it possible for downlines to show a fair profit while they are growing? Hyped-up future income projections may sound good, but people also need to be able to see results along the way.

Ask yourself whether the target levels of monthly turnover are realistic. Could they be achieved by the average person? And what are the requirements for continuing to receive commission payments on your downlines' business once they start to grow?

Look at the top people in the company — are they earning serious income from the plan? Expensive clothes and cars may give credence to any verbal claims, but do beware of the 'fake it till you make it' brigade. If someone tells you they are earning £10,000 a month, you may be wise to ask further questions rather than accepting such a claim at face value. Truly successful people do not need to boast about their income — their attitude and lifestyle should say it all for them. Beware of those who do ...

SUCCESS CHECK

The marketing plan:

★ Is it easily understood?

★ Is it simple to explain?

★ Is it possible to make a reasonable profit at the lower commission levels?

★ Are the targets for the commission levels realistic?

★ What are the requirements for continuing to receive payments on downline business?

★ Are other people earning good money from the business?

The support and training programme

The support and training programme available from the company is important for you as a newcomer to network marketing and also for all those you bring into your business. For example, if you are going to be able to sponsor people who live outside your immediate locality you will need a national network of meetings and a comprehensive training programme into which you can slot them.

Remember too that your entire downline will be more productive if they can regularly get together with other motivated people in the business. Enthusiasm breeds enthusiasm. A good upline will provide

21

the immediate field support, but it is important to look to see what input the company itself makes.

Will you have to pay for your downlines to be trained and, if so, how much will it cost? What is the quality and extent of the training? Is there a national network of training schools, or will you have to travel hundreds of miles? Does the company sponsor national and regional motivational seminars?

The availability of good literature and sales aids can also make an enormous difference to your overall success. The lack of a quality company video can seriously hamper your long-distance sponsoring efforts. Ask to see all the company literature. Does it look professional and is it worded in a way which appeals to you? Remember that, apart from you, this literature is the main spokesman for the parent company — an important factor to bear in mind when you come to share your business with others.

SUCCESS CHECK

Support and training:

★ Is there an established network of introductory meetings?

★ Is there an established network of training meetings?

★ Will you have to pay for training?

★ How much?

★ Is the company literature of good quality?

★ Is there a professionally made company video?

Financial stability

If the company is relatively young, you should ideally get a copy of their last audited accounts and study them in depth; but if you find accounting the least exciting aspect of running a business this may be a bit mind-boggling. You may know someone involved in the world of finance and accountancy; if so ask them to check the firm out for you. Alternatively, you may like to employ someone. Find out if the company is growing, declining or stagnating. What is its commitment to new investment? Does its management team have a proven track record?

If the company has been around for a few years, and has been successful, it will make a point of mentioning these points in the available literature. With most established companies, especially if they are members of the Direct Selling Association (DSA), you should not experience any problems in this area.

You may be tempted to join one of those exciting-sounding start-up companies. The potential they offer of being in at the beginning, and thus being at the top of the tree, can make the opportunities offered by the established firms seem relatively tame. But be careful. So often these bright new stars flare up, only to flicker and die in a frighteningly short time. Poor management and insufficient financial backing are often to blame.

This is not to say that you should not join a company without a track record — after all, today's multi-million pound giants were once in the same position — indeed, the rewards for being in at the beginning of a successful company can be very great. But do first weigh up the risks against the security of an established company with a history of long-term, steady growth. The choice is yours, but an important point to bear in mind is that a company's growth rate is not necessarily an indication of what your growth rate will be. Always relate the information you are given to your individual circumstances — will it work for you, is it something you feel comfortable with?

SUCCESS CHECK

Financial stability:

★ Is the company growing, stagnating or declining?

★ Is it well established, or a start-up company?

★ How much profit did they make last year?

★ Are they carrying heavy debts?

The direct selling association (DSA)

The DSA is described in Appendix B, but it is worth mentioning at this stage as several multi-level companies are members. Any DSA company should be trading in an ethical manner, and you stand a greater than average chance of such a company being financially sound. It is a good idea to write to them and take a look at what their members can offer. Make it clear that you need information on network marketing companies, as they also cater for the conventional direct sales industry.

Stay with one company

Some people manage to do more than one thing well at a time, but most of us cannot. At some point you will almost certainly be tempted to take on the products of an additional multi-level company. After all, why not double up on your profits?

The problem is that you will also double, or treble, up on your hassles. Your accounts will become more complex and the very least you will get is a headache. Sponsoring into two separate companies can become a nightmare of confusion.

But most importantly, your attention will be divided. To make this business work your mind needs to be focused. You will find that dealing with two companies can so scatter your energy that you end up selling neither particularly well. So make your choice and stick with them.

Whichever company you choose, and no matter how much market research you do, there will always be an element of risk attached to starting a business − any business. That is in the nature of the game. All you can do is minimise the uncertainty by doing some intelligent thinking and probing.

But if you don't try, you will never know what you could have achieved . . .

Network Marketing Success Story
TREVOR AND JACKIE LOWE
Eastbourne, East Sussex

Before taking up network marketing, Trevor ran his own laboratory chemical company. A biochemist by profession he had plenty of orders, but any growth was being stifled by enormous capital requirements. He was in the process of selling the business off when a friend introduced him to Amway.

Trevor immediately saw the advantages the business plan had over conventionally structured industry where he had found that the larger firms were always delaying payment to the smaller outfits, creating terrible cash-flow problems. He liked the low capital requirements of network marketing, the lack of employees and the cash with order system of doing business.

Trevor and Jackie work their business together on the principle that two heads are better than one. They work evenings and occasional weekends, with only a small amount of daytime selling. Thus they have plenty of free time to spend on voluntary work which they would not be able to pursue, but for their network marketing business.

Their main work today is in motivating and teaching other people, organising conferences and rallies around the country which attract thousands. Their success is living proof that the highest summits in the network marketing business can be scaled.

Their tips for success are first of all to choose the right company to suit you. They particularly like the consumable product range because the repeat sales give them the opportunity to develop real customers and to build up a long-term relationship with them. They also say that once you have chosen a company you will need to work hard – your investment will be in terms of time, not money.

When they first came to network marketing Trevor and Jackie made the mistake of thinking they knew all about business, having had plenty of previous experience in industry. Nothing could have been further from the truth. They tried to run their network marketing business their way, rather than the way shown by their sponsors, but it didn't work. Instead of quitting, they went back to their sponsors and discussed the problem. They learned what their sponsors had learned and applied it and hey presto, this time it worked!

They came to realise that a completely fresh mental attitude is needed to become successful in networking and that *duplication* is the name of the game.

3. RETAILING THE PRODUCT

Y OU now have an overview of what network marketing is, and an insight into some of the potential rewards. Hopefully you will now feel inspired to try for some of those dreams you previously thought were out of your reach. But you will not earn a fortune simply by dreaming of success – you must *do* something to bring it about.

The subjects covered in the next two chapters are the dual aspects of all multi-level businesses: retailing the product; and building a distribution network.

The financial return from retailing

It is important for you to decide from the start exactly what you want from your business. Do you want an extra £30 a week; or are you looking for a full-time business which will eventually provide you with a six-figure income?

If your answer is £30 a week, and you want it now, this can be achieved simply by retailing the products of your company. Anything over this sum and you would be much better off putting your energy into sponsoring other people. Retailing will provide you with immediate cash. Building a network business takes longer to show profits but brings greater rewards in the long run.

The ideal is to do both retailing and sponsoring, but for the purposes of illustration let's first assume that you only wish to retail your product and not get involved in organising and training others.

Which outlets can be used, and which cannot?

Conventional retail outlets

Many people, when first starting out, think of approaching conventional retail outlets such as shops and market stalls as a way of selling their product. Although this may work in the occasional isolated case, generally you will be wasting your time. All MLM companies insist that a single person sign their contract and that this person be responsible for the receiving and payment of moneys. This creates accounting difficulties when considering any large chain of retail stores.

Many smaller shops may seem to be lucrative targets. After all, if you signed up the owner and had him selling your product across his counter you would soon achieve a healthy turnover from just the one store, wouldn't you? Unfortunately it is not that easy. Shelf space is at a premium in any shop, and is constantly vied for by numerous manufacturer's reps. These companies often indulge in cut-throat marketing tactics to ensure that their product is displayed and not that of a rival. So you are in competition straight away with an army of hardened professional salesmen – and most multi-levellers do not come into this category.

Remember also that products are targeted towards certain markets. Many factors are considered by a manufacturer when originating a product, including price, quality, appeal, repeatability, packaging, advertising and sales literature. Your multi-level product range has, naturally, been designed to be suitable for the multi-level type of marketing approach. Network marketing companies do not advertise. They rely solely on word-of-mouth recommendations – by their distributors and by satisfied customers. As your sales literature is geared towards this word-of-mouth approach, how will you attract customers into the shop to seek your product? And how will you supply point-of-sale display stands and other material so that the shop owner can draw the attention of his customers to your products?

If you really want to sell products to retail stores you should be setting yourself up as a manufacturer's agent. But it is doubtful whether you would make as much money.

Industrial applications

Much of what has been said above applies also to the various industrial applications some products may appear to have. A large company could buy a lot of product, and the potential order value from just one commercial sale can be extremely enticing. But there is an equally huge amount of time and hassle involved in dealing with industry.

The dream of landing the 'big order' is prevalent among many who are inexperienced in the multi-level marketing business. It is good to have dreams – but this one can turn into a nightmare of wasted energy.

Your 'warm' market

So, having disposed of where you are not going to sell your products, where *do* you retail them? Simply to everyone you meet! Everybody has a circle of friends, acquaintances, work colleagues and business contacts. These people constitute what is known as your 'warm market'. Do not be concerned that you have never sold a thing in your life before; you will not be 'selling' in the accepted sense of the word.

A more apt description is that you will be *sharing* the benefits of your product with your friends and colleagues. This is often termed the 'show and tell' method. You buy the product, use it, like it and share a good thing with your friends. You show them what the product does and tell them how enjoyable you have found it to be.

Retail advertising

Let's imagine that you need a new car. How are you going to choose one from the vast range of choice available today? You may read the car advertisements in the Sunday supplements and take an increased interest in the television commercials. You will almost certainly browse around several showrooms.

But which type of advertisement would you value most of all? I suggest that if someone you knew and trusted owned a similar style of vehicle to the one you were considering buying, and told you how reliable and comfortable it was, how well it performed, etc., you would give a lot of credence to their recommendation. If, in addition, you were able to take your friend's vehicle on a test drive and you liked the feel of it, you would probably be very tempted to follow their example and buy that same model.

Personal and trusted recommendation of any product is *the* most powerful advertisement in existence. It is the foundation stone of all successful network marketing businesses. Your credibility with your friends and colleagues will be the basis for your success.

The only role for conventional advertising in the networking strategy is in the field of recruitment. Retail advertising of your product in newspapers and magazines will generally be a waste of your time and money, since you will be competing against national companies, with products similar to yours, who will be spending thousands, maybe millions, on a strategically planned advertising campaign. Can you compete with heavy artillery like this?

Profit margins and price

The profit margin on multi-level products is high because of the low overheads involved:

- there is no costly advertising;
- there are no middlemen wholesalers to cream off the profits;
- there is no necessity for expensive offices, showrooms or shops;
- there are no extra rates or rent to pay;
- there are no wages or national insurance premiums to pay;
- there are no employees to go sick and cost you money, etc.

Multi-level companies can therefore pass the profits on to their distributors. This is also the reason so many MLM products are of such high quality, as more money can be spent on research, development and quality control.

If you are looking for only minimal involvement with network building, a high value item would be a possible choice of product as the profit per individual sale is high. The amount of profit makes it worth while putting some time into each presentation. Similarly, it would also be a good choice if you wish to try working a cold market, i.e. people whom you do not know and whose interest has been aroused by some form of canvassing. The drawbacks are that you will continually have to find new customers, since repeat sales will only come when the product wears out, which will often be in several years.

But the majority of MLM products do not have a high retail sale value. If the selling price is low you need to carry several lines in order to generate a realistic level of profit, like a high street shop. One way of retailing such items is to use a catalogue passed around among friends, or distributed door to door. If you build up a round of regular customers, and service them every three months or so, this can be quite lucrative.

The party-plan approach is also a good way of retailing quantities of low-priced products to several people at the same time. Party plan used to be the exclusive preserve of housewives, but recently it has been extended to include men who are interested in such product areas as men's grooming, vitamins, jewellery, even domestic appliances.

Network building is also retailing

There is one other method of retailing products which should be mentioned here. This is simple in the extreme but can leave many people scratching their heads and asking, 'But who sells the product?' The technique can also fit under the heading of network building, but it's included here as it is also a way of moving product.

The method is simply to recruit large numbers of people into your business, who, like yourself, will use the product and then continue to reorder from the company. They will of course be buying at wholesale prices, which is of benefit to them and increases the turnover of your group. In addition they will, in the course of their normal daily lives, come across people who do not wish to sign with the company but who will buy product from them at retail prices.

By operating a combination of own use of product and a small number of retail sales to those in the immediate vicinity of yourself and your downlines, you can build a large and profitable business.

To the outsider who understands nothing of network marketing this may superficially seem like pyramid selling. But there is nothing wrong with large numbers of people obtaining a product at wholesale prices for their own use, while at the same time passing a small quantity of that product on to their friends at retail prices. This approach, with the right product, will also appeal to those people who wish to do a minimum amount of retailing and a maximum amount of recruiting and training. You will find that the majority of long established multi-level companies sell low-priced, consumable, repeat items.

SUCCESS CHECK

What you must consider about retailing:

★ you must decide how much you want to earn from retailing

★ you must decide how much actual product selling you want to do

★ the best advertisement is a personal recommendation from a satisfied customer

★ network building is also retailing

Network Marketing Success Story
JOHN CATON
Kingsthorn, Herefordshire

John Caton was previously employed as a systems programmer before going full-time with Kleneze. He became disenchanted over a period of time due to his employer's policy of increasing the work load and offering pay rises at less than inflation. But the decision to go full-time self-employed was precipitated by a visit to his parents.

John and his father went down to the pub for a pint and a game of darts. But finances were stretched to the limit and John did not even have enough money to buy his father a drink. Embarrassed, he swore from that day on he would never find himself in such dire straights again.

Having operated his Kleneze business part-time for five years John knew it was solid and secure. The company had proved itself to be honest and had never let him down. He took the plunge and has never had cause to regret his decision.

A rarity in network marketing, John obtains a large slice of his income from personal retailing. He enjoys the customer contact and the relationships he has built up over the years. He cannot see

31

himself ever not retailing, although sponsoring is starting to play an increasingly important role. One of the main strengths of Kleneze, he feels, is that a new agent can show a good profit from day one. Retailing is easy as housewives know and trust the company's name, and look forward to the next time he calls.

His tips for success are to offer a good, honest service and to build up a relationship with your customers. He treats many of his as if they were friends. Above all else though he says you need to be determined, and that the only way to start is to *get out there and do it.*

4. BUILDING A NETWORK

To make a really big income in this business there is no doubt that you need to build a network of distributors around the country. And there is no reason why you should not develop an international business. Every country where your parent company is established is your potential market-place.

By building a network of self-employed associates you can have hundreds, even thousands of people contributing to your income – but none of these will actually be employed by you.

Bear in mind as we continue that the concept of creating a multi-level income is extremely simple. In fact it is too simple for some people to accept. This is especially true of intellectuals. Unable, or unwilling, to think in simple terms they complicate it in their own minds, ending up confused – and unsuccessful. If you come across people in this category ask them to consider this statement: 'Those who sit and analyse may think themselves very clever, but those who simply work the business can end up rich ....'

The difference between conventional income and network income

There are three main income categories:

● linear income;
● residual income; and
● network income.

First, we will look at the one everyone is familiar with – *linear income*. Here you receive one day's pay for one day's work; one week's pay for a week's work, etc. Or you may get paid a set amount for each piece of work you produce. Although certain professions such as film stars, doctors, lawyers, and airline pilots may receive tremendous salaries, in general there is little scope for the creation of great wealth.

Secondly, there is *residual income*. Here your annual income builds year by year as the result of your efforts in past years. The insurance industry is a prime example. The salesperson earns a commission on all the policies he sold in previous years. If the agent has enough policies coming due, a considerable income can be earned on top of his current year sales. Song writers, musicians and authors also earn residual incomes in the form of royalties.

Then there is *network income*. People who earn network income take advantage of the efforts of others to make money for themselves. Automobile manufacturers have no financial investment in their distributor networks, who are entirely independent. Similarly, the large franchise chains such as Macdonalds, Wimpy, Body Shop, etc., utilise the resources of their independent franchisees to create enormous wealth for themselves.

There is little difference between the way the network principle is utilised by large corporations and franchisors, and the way individual networkers use it, except that the auto manufacturer will have to spend large sums of money on advertising to back up its distributor network, who will likewise have to invest thousands of pounds in showroom space and servicing facilities. Remember also that £15,000 to £250,000 is needed just to buy any form of franchise, whereas a network marketing business can be started for as little as £75, and often much less.

Duplication – the key to your success

Consider this example. Assume you have recruited a hundred people, and that each person sells or consumes £10 worth of product a month. That's £1,000. You could be receiving a commission cheque from your company each month on that entire £1,000, plus whatever you decide to retail personally. And don't forget that compared to the true performance of many in this business, we are using extremely conservative figures in this example.

The concept being illustrated here is the fundamental basis of network marketing – a lot of people each retailing and/or con-suming a small amount of product. The ratio of retailing to sponsoring may vary, but the underlying principle remains the same.

34

The numbers game

At this point many people may fight shy of the idea of attempting to work with over a hundred people. Don't worry, the greatest number of people you will ever work with directly at any one time will be five! Let's look at this in detail.

In multi-level marketing you are your own first level, or generation. This is comparable to life. If you are the first generation, your children will be your second, their children (your grandchildren) your third, and so on indefinitely.

Now, most people can handle the idea of sponsoring, or bringing into the business, two people. Those two people are your second level, or generation. If they bring in another two each, that equals four people on your third level. If those four bring in two people each there will then be eight on your fourth level. And if each of those eight brings in two there will be sixteen people running successful businesses five levels deep. These are all part of your business and you will receive commission − the amount of which depends on the individual marketing plan of your company − on the performance of them all.

Now look at what happens with only small increases in your sponsoring efforts. Imagine, instead of two people, you bring three committed people into your business and that this is replicated five levels deep. The maths looks like this:

$$3 \times 3 = 9 \quad \text{people on your 3rd level}$$
$$9 \times 3 = 27 \quad \text{people on your 4th level}$$
$$27 \times 3 = 81 \quad \text{people on your 5th level}$$

So, by bringing only one extra person into your business, and teaching them in the same way, your fifth generation now stands at eighty-one people.

If you bring in an extra two people, making four altogether, the maths now looks like this:

$$4 \times 4 = 16 \quad \text{people on your 3rd level}$$
$$16 \times 4 = 64 \quad \text{people on your 4th level}$$
$$64 \times 4 = 256 \quad \text{people on your 5th level}$$

This shows quite a staggering increase at your fifth level, doesn't it? But the real difference is only that you have sponsored another two people.

Finally we will see what the figures look like if you bring only another three people into your business. You will now have personally sponsored only five people:

$$5 \times 5 = 25 \quad \text{people on your 3rd level}$$
$$25 \times 5 = 125 \quad \text{people on your 4th level}$$
$$125 \times 5 = 625 \quad \text{people on your 5th level}$$

At this point you have a total of 780 people in your busines (5 + 25 + 125 + 625). If all these people did nothing more than order £10 worth of product for their own use each month you would be receiving commission on £7,800!

If they each had ten retail customers, that would give a total of 7,800 customers. If each of those customers purchased only £5 worth of product each month, that would give a group retail turnover of £39,000. Add that to the £7,800 which your associates are ordering themselves, and you get the staggering figure of £46,800! And, again, you can be receiving commission cheques on this entire amount. This simple example illustrates the power of recruiting, the power of network marketing.

These figures are staggering because, in the example, we are working with absurdly low figures. In reality you can sponsor many more people, and your customers will purchase much more than an average £5 a month. From this you can begin to see how incomes of £10,000 plus each and every month can be generated.

The above example is useful to show people when first introducing them to the business. You will find it helps to calm their fears that they have to personally sponsor half the country. Sponsoring five people appears a lot easier and much more plausible.

The catch

Of course, if it were as simple as the above example everyone would be a network marketing millionaire. So what is the catch? If you apply the principles contained within the pages of this book, and listen to your successful uplines, you will be successful. There is no hidden catch but there are two main difficulties which you must be prepared to overcome.

Human nature

The first difficulty is human nature. You may have to sponsor 15, 50, or even 250 people in order to find those 5 who will become as serious about the business as you are. There is no way of determining how long it will take you to find these people. What is certain is that you will need stamina to keep going while you search, and a special attitude to enable you to withstand the disappointment of those who don't make it.

That special attitude is *detachment*. You will need to be detached from the success or failure of your sponsoring efforts. You will find many people would rather suffer their problems and continue to complain about them than do anything constructive to alter their lives. If you get too wrapped up in trying to sort them out you will grind yourself into the ground. Help as much as possible, but stay emotionally detached from these people so they do not drag you down with them.

It will be hard work

The second difficulty to come to terms with is that building a successful network, like building any business, is hard work. If you come into network marketing believing it to be a get-rich-quick scheme which requires little effort, you are due for a rude awakening. Having said that, it can also be one of the most enjoyable of businesses and can provide you with a great deal of satisfaction.

● The more effort you put in, the greater the results you will get out!

The true picture

Some of you may, at this point, be doing some calculations and figuring that there are not enough people in the world to cope with the growth rates that are being talked about. Let's address that problem now and get it out of the way.

This is not an easy business. There is no point in pretending otherwise. The numerous reasons for failure are all covered somewhere in this book. You *can* be one of the success stories if you apply the knowledge contained herein. But the truth is that only a small percentage of people who start up in network marketing will actually take the trouble to apply that knowledge. The number of people who manage to make the business work the way the figures say it should is tiny compared to the numbers who try, which is, of course, a major reason why network marketing companies have survived, and continued to grow steadily, for over thirty years.

According to pure mathematical theory there could be 67,000,000 people in any one multi-level business within six months. In practice, because only a few will ever create giant networks of several thousand people, it does not happen. Another factor is that the UK birth rate is greater than the increase in distributors in any major MLM operation. The final reason, for the pragmatists among us, is that it has never yet happened!

SUCCESS CHECK

Four key principles for building a successful network:

★ you must alter the way you *think*

★ you must duplicate yourself in others

★ you must be detached from the success or failure of your downlines

★ remember that it is going to take a lot of dedicated effort before you can relax on that tropical beach

---

The benefits of network building

In all jobs and most businesses you have to keep on working. Usually, if you were to take six months' holiday in a year you would soon have to start looking for another way to earn a living – because no employer is going to keep your job open; and nearly all businesses would have collapsed.

Not so with network marketing. Once you have built your business beyond a certain size there is no way you can stop it growing, even if you wanted to. Your downlines will continue to operate their businesses regardless of whether you are around or not. You can literally be sunning yourself in the Caribbean while the cheques continue to roll into your bank account!

This aspect of the business can have an enormous impact on your life. You need never have to worry about money again, never have to be concerned about job security or constantly finding ways to keep your business afloat. You can take early retirement and participate in all those activities you dreamed of doing, but could never find the time for.

You can have time for your family, time to travel − and have the income to enjoy your leisure hours. This business also represents security for your family. In the unfortunate event of your death, your spouse and children would be able to continue to enjoy the income you have created for them. Isn't that worth the commitment of a little time and energy?

Network marketing is the great economic leveller. It doesn't matter whether you are rich or poor when you first start out. It doesn't matter if you have a hatful of degrees or have spent your life working on a building site. Everyone has the same opportunity to succeed. Indeed, a particularly apt description of the business is, 'A business for the people, and by the people.'

Of course, dreams of great magnitude cannot be realised overnight, or without the expenditure of a great deal of effort. But if you give this business three to five years of persistent hard work, enthusiasm, and commitment, you should be able to take it easy for the rest of your life. What other business or occupation can offer you rewards like that?

Think about this question. If you do not start a network marketing business *now*, and begin working towards the achievement of your dreams, where will *you* be in five years time . . . ?

SUCCESS CHECK

The benefits of creating a large network:

★ a large network will generate an enormous income for you

★ a large network gives you the option of taking early retirement

★ a large network will enable you to go on holiday and know that you will still have a business to come back to

★ a large network will give you time for travel and leisure and the money to enjoy it.

★ a large network will provide security for your family

Network Marketing Success Story
BARRY AND ANNETTE SCHOFIELD
Bracknell, Berkshire

Barry and Annette Schofield ran a door-to-door potato delivery service before coming to network marketing. At the time they were introduced to Nature's Sunshine potato prices had started to fall and their income was plummeting with them.

In most self-employed ventures if you are healthy and are able to work you can earn a decent living, but as soon as you have an accident or fall ill you can run into serious problems. Barry and Annette saw network marketing as a way to create more security. They saw that their income would build on the basis of work done in the previous months and years, and would provide money even if they both became incapacitated. As Barry was approaching fifty, concern over possible future health problems prompted them into making the change. As he says, any business which can provide a healthy income year after year without a large financial investment has got to be worth looking at.

That was in 1978. Since they made a commitment to Nature's Sunshine it has become their full-time business. With the nutritional products that the company manufactures Barry and Annette have been able to build up a substantial monthly repeating personal sales volume which comes in regardless of their own input.

When they first started in the business Barry says they had difficulty in adjusting to the drop-out rate. All direct sales operations have a high throughput of people and it took some time for them to come to terms with this. He says it is an integral part of the business which everyone has to accept. This is the reason you should spend most of your time recruiting new people – as a lot of your income will be generated by downlines who stay with you for only a short period.

Barry also drew an interesting comparison between network marketing and evangelical religions. Belief and enthusiasm help both to grow. And unless you possess these qualities yourself you are never going to be able to communicate them. He says that you must believe that what you are offering your customer is the best thing for them. You must be prepared to help others succeed. Seeing others get on, helping them and offering them a business opportunity which costs them nothing are great sources of satisfaction for Barry and Annette.

40

5. TAKING A FRESH LOOK AT SELLING

 M ANY people freeze at the mention of the word 'selling'. What images does it conjure up in your mind? Double glazing? The slick suit and the smarmy smile? Shallow friendliness? High pressure? The list could go on and on. The commonly held image of selling is that it is a method of manipulating people into buying things they do not really want to buy. But is this a completely fair picture?

Undoubtedly the archetypal salesperson did exist, and still does to some extent; but selling in the 1990s is fast becoming a much more enlightened profession. The emphasis now is on selling as a person to person liaison, as opposed to a salesman versus customer confrontation.

Network marketing is not looked on by the majority of its participants as a professional selling business in the usually accepted sense. Indeed, many distributors shy away from the word 'selling', feeling that using it will put people off.

However, many of the techniques employed by today's top salespeople *can* be used effectively in network marketing both for selling product and to increase your success in recruiting. Indeed, many of the principles of successful selling can be used to enhance our personal day-to-day communications. But what we need to do first is redefine what selling is, and just what it means to be a salesperson.

Selling is about people

In every sale there are two people − the seller and the buyer. So many people make the mistake of looking upon their prospective customer as just that − a customer, or a commodity. However, if you see

41

yourself as a sales*person*, as opposed to a salesman or saleswoman, and see your customer also as a person, then you will not only generate more sales, but you will also feel better about yourself. Your customer will also feel better about you. And customers who are happy with the product they have bought and with the person who sold it to them, are far more likely to recommend both to their friends.

Do be *sincere* in all your dealings, whether you are talking with a retail customer or a prospect for your business. There are people who walk up to someone, shake their hand, say 'Pleased to meet you,' but before that short sentence is finished they have transferred their attention to someone else. This sort of attitude is intolerably rude and most unhelpful in business.

When you speak to another person give them your full attention, look them in the eye, and *listen* to what they have to say. Do not move on to speak to someone else until you have completed your first conversation. If you show respect to others through your actions and statements they will also respect you.

Put the other person's needs first

If you were to walk into your customers' homes and say to them, 'The purpose of my visit is to make some money for myself', how do you think it would go down? Like a lead brick, wouldn't it? In fact you would be lucky not to be violently thrown out of the house, and your chances of making any sales would be almost zero. But this is the attitude that so many inexperienced salespeople adopt.

A basic axiom for business success is to find a need and then fill it. In other words you should be finding out what other people are lacking, and looking for ways to give it to them. When you stop trying to get what *you* want, and begin helping other people to get what *they* want — you will experience far more success with far less stress.

The benefits which products bestow on their owners vary dramatically according to type. The range of products sold by network marketing companies is now so vast that it is beyond the scope of this book to cover them item by item. Your company and upline will give you specific advice relating to your individual needs. The benefits of building a business are universal, however, and apply to both consumable and speciality products, so it is worth looking at some needs which are common to everybody.

The desire for money

Few people want to start up a business purely for the love of it. We all want a financial reward for our efforts. Some people will want to start part-time, just paddling their feet in the waters, while others dive straight in at the deep end and never look back. You must find out the level at which each individual wishes to work by *asking questions*.

Asking the right questions is always better than telling someone something. This principle applies across the board in selling and you should be using it all the time. If someone tells you something, there will always be room for doubt in your mind, won't there? But if you tell the other person something, you do not doubt your own words, do you? Follow this argument and you will see that when a customer answers your questions they are telling you something. Therefore, they will not doubt whatever statement they are making. But if it was you that had told them the same thing they may not believe you even if you argued with them all day.

When you have found out exactly what your prospect wants you can proceed to show them how your business can provide exactly that. Show them how they can achieve those dreams they cherish. Do not try to push someone who only wants an extra £30 a week into creating an international business generating several thousand pounds a month. Doing this can have the effect of turning your prospect off completely, if only because they cannot conceive of ever achieving such heights. Likewise, you will be wasting your time showing a successful businessman how to earn an extra £30 a week, which will probably only be an hour's work for him.

Money is an interesting subject. We will return to it later on in this chapter.

The desire for freedom

Establish if this is what your prospect is interested in by *asking* them. Then show how a network marketing business can provide more freedom than just about any other business around. Show how the repeat sales aspect will build up their retirement income; and how they can build a network of distributors from whom they will continue to earn commission even if the prospect goes on holiday. With most other small businesses it can be difficult for the proprietor to take holidays because trade then drops off so rapidly.

Point out that there are no employees and the attendant problems

43

of tax, sick pay, unions, etc, to worry about. To anyone who has been an employer this will be a big selling point.

The desire for security

What would happen in most small businesses if you, as a one-man (or one-woman) band, were to go sick or have an accident? Almost certainly your trade would diminish to zero, wouldn't it? But in a network marketing business your downlines will go on producing sales just as normal. So this business can be looked upon as a form of permanent health insurance policy. Everyone desires some form of security and this is another big plus point.

SUCCESS CHECK

The basic needs people want their business to satisfy:

★ money   ★ freedom   ★ security

At this point it may be helpful to refer back to pages 8 – 9 and 38 – 39. The information found on these pages will be useful to have at hand when talking to people about your business.

Your selling purpose

What is your true purpose in selling? Is it simply to line your pockets at the expense of your customers? Or are you in business to offer your customer a service?

If you were to put on the shoes of your customer, how would you like to be treated? What feelings would you like to be left with after the salesperson departs? Take a while to think about this. An ability to walk a mile in another person's shoes is well worth cultivating.

You would probably like to feel good about your purchase, and about yourself for having made that purchase. Few people would want to feel any other way, would they? This whole concept revolves around the principle of caring that your customer gets a good deal, not just that you will make a bundle of money out of them. This is not as altruistic as it may sound: it is, in fact, simply good business sense.

How many referrals would you give to someone you did not trust or like? And would you go into business with someone whose only interest in you appeared to be the amount of money they were going to make out of you? Most unlikely.

People will not only be buying your product, service or business plan – they will also be buying how they imagine using or implementing them will make them feel. When your attention is focused on satisfying the needs of the other person – of helping others to get what they want as opposed to trying to get what you want – you will make more sales, and will be able to bring more people into your business.

SUCCESS CHECK

Your selling purpose:

★ to help other people feel good about their purchase, and about themselves for having made the purchase

---

Do you really want money?

At first glance that may sound like a daft question. But it is an interesting one. How many people actually do want money? If you were to stop one hundred people in the street and ask them what they wanted out of life, the chances are that more money would come out on top in the majority of cases. But is this addressing the truth of the matter? Do we want more money – for its own sake – or do we want the things that money will buy?

Most people derive few good feelings about actually *possessing* money. Good feelings come from *spending* money, not hoarding it. Over and above a certain level – to provide security – the acquisition of money becomes fairly meaningless. Indeed, the majority of millionaires will tell you that their drive comes not from a desire for money, but from the excitement and challenge of creating something which previously did not exist. Several of these people have even attributed their success to having no great desire for money of itself; rather, money is something which comes as a natural result of doing other things correctly.

This is worth bearing in mind when approaching people with your business plan. You will find many successful people have no need for extra income, and even less time to pursue it. But if you probe deeper, by asking questions, you may find that they are dissatisfied with their business or career, successful though it may be. Or they may be bored by it and would welcome the challenge of building something new.

Never assume that people will want the same from the business as you do. Ask your prospect what it is that they are searching for and sell them your business as a way of satisfying that yearning.

Always be retailing

When you are dealing in speciality products you should never cease to retail product, even when you reach the top-level positions within your company. Retailing product to the end consumer is the heart of your business and what you do will be imitated by your downlines. Can you visualise what would happen if everyone in your organisation decided to play at being sales manager, putting their feet up and expecting everyone else to do the donkey work? No sales would be made and no sales equals no income. QED.

When considering consumable products the game is somewhat different, since you could decide to sign everyone into your business as a wholesale user. If you follow this route you will be, in effect, retailing and sponsoring at the same time. This system can work effectively, with the advantage that your customers can more easily be persuaded to introduce new people to the business. But it should be pointed out that most consumable orientated companies teach their distributors to create a small nucleus of around ten to twenty retail customers, and encourage them to service this nucleus once every one to three months.

Ultimately the choice is yours. Why not try it both ways and see which works best for you?

Selling your product

When you sell a customer a product, what do you tell them? Do you go on for hours about the quality of its construction and the materials from which it is made? Do you tell them about the manufacturing process and about the chemistry and physics which went into its creation? No! No! No! Your customer is not interested in most of this stuff. Your customer is only interested in what the product will do for them.

In any selling situation you must show the customer how they will *benefit* from the product. This is so important that it should be illustrated with an imaginary sales situation.

Assume that you are selling a household cleaning agent called Cleanwipe. You could say something like, 'Cleanwipe is made from the highest quality chemicals, and each batch is tested in our laboratories before it gets to you. The container is made from a special grade of plastic which took years of research and development to perfect. I really think this is the best product on the market today.'

So what is wrong with that statement? Well, you are not telling them much and you are not saying anything about what benefits the customer can expect to gain by buying Cleanwipe.

Compare it to this, 'We use the highest grade ingredients in Cleanwipe, so you can be sure there is nothing in this product which could hurt you or your children. That's an important factor, isn't it? We test each batch before it leaves the factory, so that you have the security of knowing that every bottle you buy will meet the same high standards. And the container is made from a new type of plastic which is biodegradable, as is Cleanwipe itself. You do want to protect the environment, don't you?

'The extra power of Cleanwipe will make your housework so much easier. No more rubbing away at stubborn dirt. With Cleanwipe your work surfaces will look like new with just one wipe!'

In other words, look at everything you sell to see exactly how its use will benefit the life of your customer, and then communicate those benefits.

Do not answer questions which have not been asked

Many people who are inexperienced in sales tell their customer all they know about their product, regardless of whether their customer is interested or not. Not only does this waste everyone's time, but it could actually be counterproductive if you oversell the item.

Answer only those questions which a customer asks and keep your answers short and to the point. The method of telling all, shotgun fashion, signals straight away that the salesperson is not being attentive to the actual needs of the people he or she is talking to. Tell your customer only the information he needs to know in order to place an order.

Build value

People buy when the perceived pleasure from their potential purchase outweighs the financial pain involved. You must continue to enhance the picture of your product in your customer's mind until they come to see its value (or benefits) as outweighing its cost. Your customers will only object to the price of something if they feel they are not getting value for money, or if their desire for the product is less than their desire to spend their money on something else.

The effect of price can be reduced by breaking it down to a weekly cost. For example, if Cleanwipe costs £10, lasts for a year, and has a weekly cost of less than 20p, and you say something like, '20p a week for a product of this quality is tremendous value for money, isn't it?', your customer will have a hard time contradicting you.

Similarly, many multi-level products cost more than their high street competitors, but last longer, making them cheaper in the long run. For example, if your competitor, Cheapclean, costs only £5, it may seem to your customer to be a better buy. But if you work out that they will need to buy four bottles of Cheapclean for every one bottle of Cleanwipe you can show them a saving of £10 a year. Again, you would be able to say, 'That's good value, isn't it?' But in this case don't break it down to weekly figures, since a saving of 20p a week is not going to excite anyone.

Notice the use of the phrase 'isn't it' at the end of each statement of benefit. You need to get your customer on your side, to get them into the habit of agreeing with you and saying 'yes', which is crucial when we come on to the next section.

Ask for the order

People buy because they feel confident in the product and the salesperson − and because they are asked to! This may be stating the obvious, but it is surprising how many people wait for the customer to ask them to sell them something. Unfortuantely life just isn't like that, however much we may like it to be so.

The best and most often used method of asking for the order ('closing' to the professionals), is to offer your customer a choice of two alternatives − the 'alternative close'. People generally find it difficult to make decisions. As a salesperson your job is to make that decision-making process easy and painless.

If you say, 'How would yo like to pay?', the poor customer has a lot of options available. He will be thinking, 'Should I pay by cheque, cash, credit card, bank loan, borrow the money off Aunt Jane, etc?'. But if you say, 'How would you prefer to pay, by cheque or by cash?', their task is made a lot easier. Here you are assuming that the customer has decided to buy. You do not actually ask directly, 'Would you like to buy a bottle of Cleanwipe?'. Too often the answer to such a question will be a 'no thanks', or 'I'll think about it'. If anyone tells you they are going to 'think about it', this is usually only a polite way of saying no. Count them as a no-sale. If they do come back to you then consider it a bonus.

The same principle of 'alternative closing' applies to asking for an appointment to see someone. You could say, 'Would sometime next week be OK?' That is pretty general and gives your prospect seven days to juggle around in their mind. But if you say, 'Would Tuesday at 9.00pm or Thursday at 7.00pm be better for you?', their decision-making process is considerably simplified.

Use this technique all the time, even in non-business situations, and you will find it makes life flow a lot smoother.

Ask for referrals

Most people like to share a good thing with their friends. You can use this basic human attribute to expand your business. You could say to your customer, 'You enjoyed using Cleanwipe, didn't you? Would you like your friends to benefit from it too? Great! I'll write down their names and telephone numbers so I don't forget, and contact them in the next couple of days.' By asking for referrals you will gain several new names, all of which could become customers. And one or two could become as enthusiastic as you about network marketing.

Even those prospects who did not buy the first time you talked to them should be contacted at frequent intervals. Don't try to sell to these people, simply ask them for referrals. Of course, you may well find that your prospect's circumstances change and they find themselves in a position to buy. This will become obvious as the conversation progresses, as long as you stay alert to what the other person is telling you.

SUCCESS CHECK

Retailing:

★ sell the benefits of your product

★ only tell your customers what they need to know in order to place an order

★ build up the value of your product

★ ask for the order

★ ask for referrals

Always be sponsoring

Changing circumstances are an important factor to remember when prospecting for people to join your business. There are successful networkers who were introduced to the concept up to four times before finally taking the plunge. Because of work, family or other commitments, they were not in a position to do anything when approached before, or sometimes the company or products they were shown did not appeal. For whatever reason, they did nothing. But when approached for the fourth time everything was right and they soared. So never eliminate someone just because you know they have not been interested in the past.

Credibility

In network marketing you trade on your credibility as a person. The extent to which others trust and believe you will have a tremendous bearing on your ultimate success. Your own belief in yourself, your own inner certainty that your product or business is right and good for the other person will give them the confidence to buy.

The three foot rule

This rules states that whenever you get to within three feet of another person, you talk to them about your business. Remember that almost everyone can be prospected. Even if you are selling a product like cosmetics you can still approach men, because men have wives and girlfriends. The main point is to look beyond the person who is facing you and see the scores, possibly hundreds, of people to whom they can introduce you. Always look for referrals, whether you are retailing or prospecting for downlines.

Conversation, needs, solution

When you meet someone for the first time, what do you talk about? If you are stuck for words simply involve them in *conversation* about their family, their work and perhaps what they do for a hobby. By discussing these things, and by asking pertinent questions, you can find out what their *needs* are. Perhaps they have a large family and express a need for more money. Perhaps they are successful, but dissatisfied with their job or existing business. Or maybe they would like nothing better than to spend more time on their leisure activities.

Then, when you have established a rapport, hit them with your *solution*, ie how you can satisfy their needs by introducing them to your network marketing business.

Feel, felt, realised

The following technique is to be used when people come up with objections about your business. One of the most common objections is that network marketing is just pyramid selling. A conversation could go like this:

'I don't want anything to do with pyramid selling rackets.'

'I know how you *feel*', you answer, 'because I *felt* that way at first as well. Then, after I had looked into the business in more depth, I *realised* that it was a perfectly legitimate means of distributing product. The problem was that I had got today's respectable and ethical network marketing companies confused with the rogue outfits which were around in the 1960s and early 1970s.'

The technique is that first you create an agreement by saying that you know how the other person feels. Secondly, you create empathy by telling them that you felt that way at first. Finally, you explain what made you change your mind. Like all good things this is both simple and effective. Check back to page 5 to see how it was used as part of the opening to this book.

We *can make a lot of money*

When you are talking to a prospect for your business you should never say, 'I think *you* can make a lot of money from this business.' You would be much better off saying, 'I really feel that *we* can make a lot of money from this business.'

The difference is that by saying 'you' it sounds as if you are out to make money off his back, but by saying 'we', you are including the other person in a joint enterprise involving them. How would *you* prefer to be treated?

SUCCESS CHECK

Sponsoring:

★ your *credibility* gives your customer *confidence*

★ remember the three foot rule

★ conversation, need, solution

★ feel, felt, realised

★ *we* can make a lot of money

Objections

It is important that you learn to see objections as a statement of interest. Your customer is telling you that they are interested, but that they need more information before they might feel able to buy. Someone who is not interested would not ask any questions or raise objections.

Objections are best disposed of before they ever arise. For example, many people express concern about the lack of territorial rights. But if, *before* they raise the objection, you say, 'Did you know that there aren't any areas in network marketing? Isn't that tremendous! It means we are free to work wherever we want without geographical restrictions', you will have neutralised the power of the objection.

So, by pre-empting the objection you have effectively killed off any objections concerning the lack of exclusivity. See solutions, not problems.

> ## SUCCESS CHECK
>
> Objections:
>
> ★ an objection is a statement of interest
>
> ★ an objection is a customer telling you they need more information
>
> ★ an objection is best disposed of before it arises

Your personal success story

Understanding how the business is working for you is an important part of your prospect's decision-making process. Therefore, you should spend some time developing a convincing testimonial to your success. This should take the form of a little story, drawn from your own experience in network marketing, illustrating how *you* have benefited from the business. Tell this story to each prospect to lend both credence and the personal touch to your presentation.

Information communicated via an interesting story is always more easily digested than straight facts and your listener will be likely to pay far more attention to what you have to say. But it is important to always be honest and sincere in everything you say. It is not worth exaggerating or lying in order to impress people, since sooner or later you will be found out. And, once you have been caught lying on one issue, you will have no credibility on anything else, no matter how hard you try to convince people otherwise.

Here are some reasons for becoming involved which you could include in your initial success story:

● your company, its age, growth rate, financial standing, etc;
● your product line;
● the support and training you have received;
● your company's marketing plan.

Once you have a track record to show people, you can then add:

● the amount of money you have made (note that an intimation that you are comfortably off is subtler than a boastful announcement that you made £X,000 last month);

- the ease with which you have sold the products;
- your position within the company;
- the number of people you have already sponsored into your business;
- how well your existing downlines are doing;
- the goals you have accomplished.

Add a few more of your own, but whatever you say, keep it brief. Remember that your prospects will be mostly interested in themselves, not in listening to a monologue of your successes. So keep your success story simple, concise and preferably no longer than one minute in duration.

The caring sales person

If there is one single point which should be emphasised in this chapter, it is the value of *caring* about your customers as people. If you care more about your customer getting value for money, superb service and a proper follow up, than you do about the profit you will make from the sale, then you will be able to build a strong business with firm foundations.

This same philosophy holds true for working with your downlines and helping their businesses to become more profitable. If you devote your time to helping other people to become successful, you cannot fail to become successful yourself.

Your *attitude* is your most important business asset and can make the difference between succes or failure. Care about all the people in your business, whether they are customers or downlines. See them as real human beings just like yourself − not objects from which to make money − and you will reap the rewards of your efforts a thousand times over.

Network Marketing Success Story
TOM HASKINS
Bristol, Avon

Tom Haskins had been involved in traditional direct selling for several years before coming into network marketing. In fact he used

54

to be totally against the entire concept, believing, as many do, that it was a con similar to pyramid selling or chain letters. It was only when he received a telephone call from a friend that he began to see the light.

After studying the company marketing plan, he saw that there was the potential for considerably greater income using network marketing techniques than there was in carrying on simply as a salesman. Tom says that the principles of network marketing had never been explained to him before in a clear, concise and logical manner. Over the years several people had tried to put the idea across to him, but either they had not fully understood it themselves, or were unable to communicate what they knew.

One of the major problems Tom had in coming to terms with networking was the lack of exclusive areas. Previously he had always insisted on territorial rights from any company with which he was involved. But his philosophy is that for every negative there is a positive and, when his friend sat down with him and went through the business step by step, he soon realised that he was sacrificing Bristol in order to gain the entire world! Needless to say he no longer sees the lack of geographical areas as a problem.

Tom continues to make retail sales as well as building a network of distributors. He likes the low-key 'try it, you'll like it' approach to selling. He sells water treatment systems – speciality products – and enjoys the freedom to be able to offer the people he sponsors the choice of either retailing the product only, or of both retailing and building a business. He sees service to his retail customers as being of paramount importance, since without a solid retail sales base he would not have the successful business he has today.

Tom chose his present company because of the quality of their product, and for their professional expertise and back-up support. His tips for success are to know your product, know your company, and not to 'stitch anyone up' – in other words to treat everyone, whether customer or business associate, in an honest and ethical manner.

Like all successful network marketing entreprenuers Tom places commitment and persistence on top of the list of qualities everyone should develop. In his own words, 'This is all I do. I don't play at this business.'

6. STARTING WITH A SUCCESSFUL ATTITUDE

ONE of the major problems you will come up against when considering network marketing is the way your mind has already been conditioned. Most of your schooling has geared you towards getting a job, or following a career path. You have been taught to strive for achievement solely through your own efforts. We have all been subjected to a subtle brainwashing and only rarely does anyone manage to break out of this restrictive mould.

Those who are already self-employed have gone some distance towards achieving a degree of freedom. But even those who manage their own companies will normally see others as only their employees. What is needed to succeed in network marketing is a radically different outlook on work and on your working relationships with others. You actually need to change the way you think.

Your *attitude* is possibly the largest single factor which will determine your success or failure in network marketing. It has been said that people with great attitudes talk about ideas, while people with mediocre attitudes talk about things and events, and those with small-minded attitudes talk about other people! If you learn to replace negative attitudes such as criticism, condemnation and complaint with positive attitudes such as conviction, courage and commitment, you will go a long way down the road towards making your dreams come true.

Network marketing businesses cost £75 or less to start up. This is great so far as an easy entry into the business is concerned; but if you are not careful this same factor can defeat you. Ask yourself this – if you had just invested £250,000 in a fast-food franchise – what attitude would you take to your business?

Probably, 99.99 per cent of people would treat such a decision very seriously. They would work all the hours necessary to ensure the success of their business. They would commit large amounts of energy to making their business work. And they would not expect to make a fortune overnight.

Compare your feelings about this hypothetical £250,000 franchise to your feelings about investing £75 in a network marketing business. Do you feel the same urgency? There is not the same fear of great losses if you were to fail. There is not the same degree of internal push which will make you want to make sacrifices to ensure the success of your business.

So, before you do anything, the important point to digest is this:

SUCCESS CHECK

★ **The attitude you need to take toward your network marketing business is exactly the same as you would adopt if you had invested a quarter of a million pounds in it.**

Treat your business as a business and you will have gone a long way towards earning a fortune. But if you take the attitude that it only cost you £75 to get in, treat it as a £75 business, and that is exactly what you will have − a £75 business.

Do you *really* desire financial and business success?

That may sound like a strange question. But the fact is that many people don't! Consider for a moment what large-scale success will mean to you and the changes it will bring into your life:

● you will have more responsibilities, because other people will be looking to you for help and guidance;
● you will have to cope with more stress because of your increased responsibilities;
● your life will become more complex simply because you are *doing* more;

● you will have more to lose because your money will have enabled you to buy more possessions;

● you could become a target for the jealousy and envy of others, sometimes from people you previously considered to be your friends. Money and success will definitely alter the way many people act towards you.

As you are already reading this book it is a safe bet that you are willing to accept the consequences of success. But it is worth considering that many people to whom you show your business will not be of the same opinion.

The psychology of success is a study in its own right and will be dealt with in Chapter 7. You will find that an understanding of human psychology will pay dividends when you begin identifying, and then working with, productive downlines. But for the moment we will look at some of the other factors that success will introduce into your life.

SUCCESS CHECK

Success will give you:

★ the freedom to organise your life the way *you* want

★ the money to enable you to enjoy your freedom

★ an improved self-image as you experience the rewards of success

★ the ability to travel further and more frequently

★ lots of new friends

★ more time for your family, social and spiritual life

Remember, as you read, that what you are learning is not only for your benefit, but is also for you to pass on to the people whom you bring into the business. The advice in this book will, correctly applied, enable you to build your business on firm foundations which will withstand the occasional flurry of stormy weather.

The successful person does – the unsuccessful person tries to do

Try this little experiment. First, consider these three statements:

- I'm trying to be successful
- I am successful
- I'm not successful

Now, sit at a table and place a book in front of you. Run through the following actions:

- Open the book
- Don't open the book

Of course, you can see the difference between 'opening the book' and 'not opening the book'.

- Now *try* to open the book

Which does 'trying to open the book' look most similar to – 'opening the book', or 'not opening the book'? Now look back at those first three statements. Do you see how 'I'm trying to be successful' and 'I'm not successful' are exactly the same?

'I am successful' is a completely different concept. 'Trying' and 'not doing' amount to the same thing. Doing equates to action, which in turn produces results. Again, we have come back to the question of attitude and the way you think. How you think has a tremendous effect on your ability to succeed.

Know where you are going – create goals

Imagine you are about to set out on a journey by boat. You need to know where you are headed before you know which course to steer. Of course you could sail around aimlessly, go nowhere in particular and come home again. That's fine if you have no desire to reach an objective. But if you want to sail from Dover to Calais you need to know that that is what you want to do! It would be senseless to set out heading towards Cornwall, then go across to Brittany, then back over to Bournemouth, etc.

But, amazingly, some people do just that when starting out in network marketing. A vague idea of what you want from your business is really not good enough. If you don't know where you are going, how will you know when you've arrived?

All successful people create, and then attain, goals. In 1952 Harvard University in the USA began a study. They took that year's graduating class and asked them how many students had written down their goals. The figure was 3 per cent.

Twenty years later that same 3 per cent had a greater net worth than the other 97 per cent combined. Their goals had changed over the years as their lives had changed, but they had always kept a written list of those things they wanted to achieve.

Here are some of the advantages of having goals:

- Goals impart a sense of purpose to your actions. They give you your 'reason why'. Few of us are born with any degree of self-motivation. Goals give you soemthing to aim for.
- Goals help you to create time for your business each day.
- Goals enable you to monitor your progress as you achieve one target after another.
- Goals increase your feelings of self-worth and improve your self-image. As you progressively achieve one goal after another, and you come to realise the extent of your accomplishments, you will feel good about yourself and what you are doing.
- Goals help boost your self-confidence. As you achieve each goal that you set yourself, your confidence that you can achieve your next goal will increase.
- Lastly, all the above factors will combine to increase your income!

How to create your goals

Decide what you really want out of life

Until you know what you want, how can you set about achieving it? Interestingly, when we sit down to contemplate our future seriously, the things we so often say we want don't seem so attractive any more. An example of this might be a desire to win the pools. Many people, if they are really honest, do not want to win the jackpot, simply because they would not know what to do with the money or the leisure time it would bring.

So think deeply about what you want from this business. Then set your goals accordingly.

Set short, medium, and long-term goals

If you only set yourself targets which will take years of work to achieve you will more than likely become disillusioned before you accomplish them. Self-confidence comes largely from succeeding at what you do. If your only goal is so high and distant that it would take Superman ten years to bring it to fruition you will be in for a lot of heartache.

You do need those expansive, long-term goals, of course. They are the stars you steer by. When the going gets tough — as it will from time to time — you need to have something distant to work towards to help give a sense of purpose to your endeavours.

But you must create smaller, more easily attainable goals too. Decide on how much you want from your business this month, and then next month. What will you buy with the money? Give yourself something concrete to aim for and which can be achieved in the near future. These short-term goals will encourage you because you will soon actually be seeing the results of your efforts. This is important. Remember also that your downlines will need to see quick results from their businesses in order for them to maintain their enthusiasm.

Medium-term goals are exactly as they sound. They will help you develop stamina. After working your business for six months it will feel good to see that you have achieved an objective which once seemed alarmingly distant. The achievement of these mid-range goals will help to sustain your belief that you can bring about the realisation of those really big dreams.

Some of the goals you need to set are as follows.

- The amount of money you want to earn.
- The purpose you will use your money for.
- The amount of time you are going to allocate to your business. You will not create a six-figure income in your first year by working only five hours a week.
- The number of prospects you are going to talk to about your business each day. If you only talk to two people each day, that means you will have presented your business fourteen times in one week. That's 728 times in one year! Does it seem reasonable that, by the law of averages, out of that number of people you should sign up several good downlines?
- The number of distributors you want to have, and when.
- Your target dates for making the various levels on the company commission schedule.

If you work steadily you will achieve your desires. The big money is not made by people who go at their businesses like a bull at a gate, but by those who take the time to plan their work — and work their plan. If you were building a house and laid only one brick a day, eventually you could still end up with a forty-room mansion. So work consistently.

Don't be a slave to your goals, however. If experience proves that you have set yourself targets which are unattainable, then adjust your goals downwards. Be realistic. Conversely, if you are achieving your goals with little effort you need to set your sights higher. Be flexible. The tree which does not bend with the wind soon comes crashing to the ground.

What to do with your goals

- *You must write yours goals down*. This solidifies your thoughts into a material form. It is always good to link mental and physical actions. Constant referral to your written list of goals will cement them in your mind.

- *You must be specific*. A vague idea like 'I want a big car' will not do. Your mind brings material things into your life only when instructed accurately. There is a saying among computer programmers — if you feed garbage into a computer, you get garbage out! The mind can be paralleled with a computer, albeit an organic one. You need to be as specific when feeding your mind as the programmer has to be when writing his program.

- *You need to give yourself time-related tasks*. Set yourself specific dates by which you expect to have achieved your goals. This imparts a sense of urgency to your actions and the time factor will give you something to race against.

- *You must visualise your goals*. The images you hold in your mind, of where you want to go and what you want to achieve, are of great importance. Your physical life is a reflection of those thoughts you hold most strongly and consistently in your mind. See Chapter 7 for more on this subject.

SUCCESS CHECK

Working with goals:

★ decide what you really want

★ decide on short, medium, and long-term goals

★ write your goals down

★ be specific

★ give yourself deadlines

★ visualise your goals

Start in a businesslike manner

Working from home

Working from home is not the easiest of disciplines. A seemingly blissful existence, the problems only come to light when you actually try doing it. The aim of this section is to point out potential dangers to those who have never been self-employed before, and to polish up the working practices of those who have.

The business attitude

Your network marketing business is just that – a business. Many people fail simply because they don't take their business seriously enough. Every successful business has to keep a close check on its finances, know where every penny is being spent and coming from, and organise itself for the most productive use of its time. And this includes you and your business.

Accounts, tax and national insurance

As a network marketing distributor you are classed as self-employed. This means you will have to pay a national insurance contribution when your profits reach a certain figure. You will also have to declare all the money you make to the tax man.

If you contact your local tax office they will shower you with explanatory pamphlets. Likewise, you local DSS office will give you details of all your national insurance obligations. Ask for their help. These people are usually very understanding to those who are just starting up in business. Make use of them.

If you intend to build a large and successful business, the use of a good accountant is strongly advised. Their fees are quite reasonable and they will take all the worry off your shoulders. You can then spend the time you would have spent in doing your accounts running your business. An accountant may even be able to save you money through his or her detailed knowledge of the tax laws.

You can use an exercise book for simple 'in' and 'out' records, but once you begin to turn over a decent amount you will need something more professional. It is better to do this from the beginning and thus start in the same professional way you intend to continue. If you are going to use an accountant buy the record-keeping book he or she prefers, such as the Simplex system, which is straightforward and workable.

The minimum you must do is keep clear records and receipts of every expense incurred for the business, and every penny you receive as income. The difference, of course, is your profit. Remember to keep a receipt whenever you buy petrol, stationery and stamps, pay your telephone and heating bills, etc. Bundle them into envelopes so that you can easily prove your expenses should the taxman ask you to.

Business bank account

It is important that you keep your business and personal finances separate. If you do not you will eventually end up in a complete muddle and it will cost you a lot in time and accountants' fees to sort it all out. It is much easier to start off correctly and avoid the hassle.

Make an appointment with your bank manager to discuss what the bank has to offer and, unless you are already sinking beneath a heavy overdraft, they will be pleased to open a separate account for your business.

Organise yourself

Ideally, you will be able to have a portion of your house set aside for your business. Here you can keep your stock, telephone and accounts. Be aware, however, that sole use of a room for business can introduce problems with captial gains tax. The minimum you must do is allocate a drawer to your business, and organise it so that you can put your hands on the correct piece of paper at the time when you want it. The time wasted, and frustration caused, by searching for information which you need but cannot find will more than offset a little time and thought put into creating an efficient flling system.

Avoiding distractions

Working from home brings with it an enormous amount of freedom. But if you don't get into the habit of working at set periods of the day, it can easily become the freedom to do nothing.

Developing the self-discipline to work when the family want to go on a picnic, the sun is shining and there is no boss to force you to do otherwise, can sometimes come painfully! But it is something you *must* do.

It must be said that there is no easy way of doing this. It comes hard to most people. What is true is that your desire to be successful must be greater than your desire to slump in front of the television after a day's work. Only a powerful, self-motivating desire will give you the will-power to go out and work your business when more immediate pleasures are beckoning.

The good side of all this is that when you have conquered your laziness a few times your mind begins to resist less and less. When you have triumphed for long enough you will find that it has re-programmed itself actually to look forward to running your business.

SUCCESS CHECK

How to be businesslike:

★ treat network marketing as a business

★ employ an accountant

★ keep clear and comprehensive accounts

★ separate personal and business money

★ do the most important things first

★ avoid distractions

Dealing with isolation

Unlike many other forms of self-employment, in network marketing you are never entirely alone. Remember that you are in business *for* yourself, but not *by* yourself.

If the blues do get to you from time to time − and it happens to the best of us − give your upline a ring. Tell them how you feel and the problems you are experiencing. They will talk you through it and soon you will wonder what you were feeling down about. That is one of the responsibilities of an upline. Do remember never to express any negativity to your downlines. This would effectively torpedo your business as you would dampen their enthusiasm and introduce doubts into their minds.

The person who will be successful is set apart from the mass of humanity by several factors which are covered somewhere in this book. But perhaps the single most important difference is the fact that successful people *do*, whilst the unsuccessful are still thinking.

Network Marketing Success Story
SIMON WEBB
Byfleet, Surrey

Simon Webb's previous job was as a service engineer. He enjoyed the work, but increasing mortgage rates were crippling him. He was faced with two alternatives: give in and sell his house; or fight and create an increased income. He chose to fight.

Simon considered starting other, more conventional businesses, but the responsbility of providing for his family and paying the mortgage precluded these. One of the major attractions of network marketing was that it required only a small amount of risk capital and could be tested out part-time.

One of the most important tips that Simon gives is to copy your successful upline leaders. When he first started in the business he had no experience of sales. So he sat down with his upline and picked her brain for knowledge which could help him to navigate the, for him, uncharted waters of network marketing.

He says that you should *never* show anyone any negatives. Even if you are feeling absolutely lousy yourself, never pass on that feeling to your downlines. Always act positively with everyone around you. If you don't, and your downline business becomes infected with your negativity, that business will slowly disintegrate. Interestingly, Simon has noticed that negative talk rebounds on himself and makes *him* feel bad whenever he has indulged in it.

By talking to several successful people, and listening to their advice and success stories, the principles of network marketing took root in his mind. He came to realise that none of these people had any more by way of special talents than he did, so he adopted the attitude of, 'if they can do it, so can I'.

7. APPLYING THE PSYCHOLOGY OF SUCCESS

WITHOUT the correct mental attitude the chances of becoming successful are slim. But the power of the mind to affect changes over our physical environment is now becoming more accepted. The greater your acceptance of this power, and the more you apply it to your life, the greater will be your chances of making your dreams come true.

We will assume that your desire is to earn an extra £30 a week from this business – and that you achieve it. If you are satisfied with that achievement, then you are successful. But if you were secretly nurturing a longing for £500 a week, you are not successful. In other words you are only truly successful if you achieve those goals on which you have set your heart. The true failures in life are not those who desire little, but those who desire much yet achieve little.

Success means different things to different people. If your desire is to do nothing with your life other than earn sufficient money to live on, have an average house, and go on holiday for two weeks a year – and that is truly what you want in your heart – then do it. Conversely, if you desire to live in a mansion and to travel the world for six months of every year – and this is truly your desire, not just a fanciful whim – then you should take the brakes off your life and fulfil your dream. Neither course of action is intrinsically better than the other. They are different, that's all. Doing that which makes you happy, doing it well, and being satisfied with your achievement is what equates to a successful life.

But within many of us are psychological barriers which must be overcome before we can be successful to any degree. One of the largest mental blocks to achieving anything is fear. Extreme fear can paralyse you into inaction; and that is not as uncommon as it may at first seem . . .

Fear

Fear can manifest itself in several ways. It is quite natural to experience a certain apprehension when starting any new project. After all, you will be coming into contact with a number of people you have never met before, and will have to absorb a quantity of new information. You wouldn't be human if you did not feel some form of tension simply at the thought of what you are going to be doing. Even the greatest actors get stage fright; Formula One racing drivers frequently cannot talk to anyone immediately before a race because they are so tense; and many eloquent public speakers never lose that initial trepidation they feel when beginning a talk.

The important point − and its importance cannot be over-emphasised − is that although these people experience a degree of fear, they are in control of that fear. It does not rule their lives.

Fear can be a life-saving factor. It serves a real and necessary purpose, and you will never be entirely rid of it. Fear enables us to survive in a hostile and dangerous world. Soldiers who felt no fear would walk calmly up to the enemy's guns − and be cut to pieces in the crossfire. But most soldiers going into battle will feel fear, and that fear will cause them to take actions and make decisions which may save their lives. It is the exaggerated, unhelpful fear which we are concerned about here.

It is often said that the hardest door to get through is your own. We will now take a look at the reasons behind this, and at the types of fear you will most commonly come across when starting your business.

The fear of failure

Those who never attempt anything, never fail at anything! Of course, the easy option is to spend your evenings staring at the television, living your life vicariously through other people's dreams. Not for you will be the humiliation of having tried and failed; not for you the financial loss incurred − and not for you will be the rewards and glory of success.

Those who never take the risk of venturing through their own front door will never see their own dreams realised, and will never have the satisfaction of creating something new. An action which fails can also be called a mistake. If you learn from those mistakes, and continue to put one foot in front of the other as you follow your chosen path, you must eventually be successful.

If you look at the lives of most successful people you will find that they have often made a greater than average share of mistakes. Look at Jeffrey Archer for example. He was a millionaire businessman who lost all his money and ended up nearly half a million pounds in debt. What did he do? Did he give up in despair, thinking that life would never work for him? No! He sat down and wrote a novel. And another. Then another. His third book, not his first as many believe, became a smash-hit bestseller. After reading *Kane and Abel* people went back to the first two books and made them bestsellers too. It took seven years for Jeffrey Archer to pay off all his debt. But by then he had made another million.

The fear of rejection

In a life of selling you will face a lot of 'nos'. Your attitude towards this constant rejection will shape the whole future of your business. I know, there can never have been anyone so frightened of rejection than myself. When I first went into sales I was totally lacking in confidence as far as talking to strangers was concerned.

My first sales job was in the arduous field of door-to-door selling. I still have a vivid memory of standing at the garden gate of the first house I was to call on. I can still feel the way my knees shook with fear! But I was strongly motivated. I had been forced to resign from my old job because of a back injury, had no money and a wife and two young children to support. After wandering the streets, trying to find the 'best' house to call on, and generally finding ways to waste time and put off the moment of truth, I finally walked up that long path to the door bell.

What did I find? An ogre with two heads? A fierce giant who wanted to eat me for his supper? No. I found an ordinary, pleasant, intelligent human being. Well, well, well. My fears had been unjustifiably blown up out of all proportion in my own imagination.

Of course I got rejected, over and over again. But some people said 'yes'. Some people bought my products, and those who did not would often refer me to someone who was interested. I came to understand the law of numbers which states that every 'no' brought me closer to a 'yes'.

Eventually, you will learn how to detach yourself from the hurt of people saying 'no'. When you learn not to take their dismissal personally, when you see the whole situation in a clear light unclouded by *imaginary* fears, you will become extremely proficient at selling.

Action is the antidote for fear. You will find that the more you confront the thing of which you are afraid, the less will that fear exert its stranglehold on your life. If you continually do something of which you are afraid and remain in control of that situation – even if you are screaming inside – your brain will build up a store of success-oriented memories. The next time you enter a similar situation your mind will be able to draw on those success memories and will feed you confidence instead of paranoia.

The fear of what others might think

Which is of greater concern to you: what others may, or may not, think about your business venture – or the realisation of your dreams?

No matter what you do, or do not do, there will be some people who wish you well, and some who will not. If the negative opinions of other people are of concern to you, you must learn to turn yourself off from them.

Some people, unable or unwilling to create successful lives for themselves, delight in destroying others' hopes as well. They will do this by making disparaging remarks about your company, its products and the marketing plan. In effect, these people are attempting to steal your dream away from you. If you allow these negative people to invade your space often enough, some of those poisonous seeds may take root, and before you know it your enthusiasm for your business will have died.

Ask yourself a few simple questions:

- Is the company I am with, or considering, reputable?
- Do the products and/or service offer good value for money?
- Is the company financially sound?

If your answer is positive on all three counts then be proud of your company, be proud of your products and be proud of yourself.

It is a natural law of life that like attracts like. If you have negative people in your circle of friends, and you maintain a strong positive attitude, you will find such people gradually dropping away from you. Successful people surround themselves with other positive people who have the same vision.

The fear that you lack sufficient knowledge

Wisdom comes from experience. Knowledge comes from learning. Neither will come about unless you *do* something. Take a look at the successful people in your business — they were all once in the same position as you are now. They were not born with their knowledge of how to build a successful business — they gained it by working their business.

If you do not know something, what are your alternatives? You can lie, bluffing your way through and hoping that you will not be exposed. You can say you don't know and leave it at that. Or you can say you don't know and promise to get back to the questioner with an answer as soon as you can.

If you follow that first route you will eventually be exposed as a fraud. You can fool some of the people some of the time, but not all of the people all of the time. And, unless you are totally without morals, you will have some difficulty sleeping at night.

If you simply say that you don't know and then shut up, how impressive will that be?

But if you say that you don't know, and promise to get back to your customer with an answer within a short time, what will be their reaction? Most people will be impressed with your sincerity and you will create goodwill. The customer will feel that you *care* about them and you will have gained valuable knowledge which will be at your fingertips the next time that question is raised. Never, ever, be ashamed of admitting that you don't know something.

In the early days of your business you will not know all the answers. How could you? If you focus on your strengths and what you can do, and not on your weaknesses and what you cannot, you will grow in confidence. And if you ask your upline for help you will receive all the support you need. Never forget that you are in business for yourself, but not by yourself. In network marketing you are never alone.

SUCCESS CHECK

Fear:

★ you will never succeed if you never run the risk of failing

★ confidence comes from the experience of successful activity

★ don't let anyone steal your dream

★ the only stupid question is the one that wasn't asked

The importance of your imagination

As you get to know the successful people in your business you will come to realise that most of them do not have any special talent or ability which you do not possess. Successful people are generally ordinary people who have been consistent in using their time and energy, and who have persistently chipped away over a period of time until the rewards came flooding back to them.

You will realise that if they can do it, so can you. And interestingly, when your own labours begin to show fruit, you will find others adopting the attitude of 'if *you* can do it, so can they'!

One of the most important success rules to follow is to take command of your mind and therefore your life. Many people take positive thinking to mean nothing more than developing their will-power. But, although a strong, positive will is to be admired, you will not achieve much in the way of results using your will alone. And what you do achieve will be hard won.

For the rest of this chapter we will concentrate on how physical circumstances are affected by that part of our mind which has often been overlooked, or ignored, as being of little importance. An understanding of that faculty called imagination, when combined with the correct application of certain other principles of life, is at the root of learning how to alter your physical circumstances.

The principles of creativity

Absolutely everything which man has built throughout history was first conceived in someone's mind. Take a while to think about it and you will see that this is true.

It stands to reason, then, that before you can create a successful network marketing business, you need first to create it in your mind. But how?

The esoteric principles which govern the creation of the universe are outside the range of a work of this nature. Fortunately it is not necessary to have an understanding of *why* life works in a certain way in order to become successful, only to know *how* it works. All you need to do is consistently apply a few fundamental principles. A train of events will then be set in motion which will result in the achievement of your most heartfelt ambitions.

Visualise your goals

By now you should have written down a list of your short, medium, and long-term goals. Spend some time forming a mental image of what your life will be like when they have been accomplished. See your house, car, lifestyle, or whatever your goal is. See it all in colourful detail. Put yourself in the picture. See yourself actually living the reality of your dreams.

Detail, colour, action, the personal touch – all these add to the power of your image, and the more powerful your imagination, the greater will be your success. Use photographs from magazines to help your imagination along. Concentrate gently on these pictures. The ideal is to constantly hold the image of what you desire in the forefront of your mind. In the beginning you will probably find your attention wandering, so start off by doing it as regularly as possible, preferably at least once a day.

Keep your goals in your mind in the form of mental images and live with them so much that they become a second world for you. Don't try too hard to create these pictures. The process really is very simple. Children do it easily and naturally, and in many ways this child-like state of mind is what we should be aiming to recapture. Too much effort creates tension; and too much tension kills imagination.

Feel that your goals are already accomplished

Feeling that your goals have already been accomplished is the intermediate step between the first mental concept and their eventual physical materialisation. Why do you have to feel that they have already been achieved? Why can't you just feel that they will come true in the future?

The simple answer to this is that tomorrow never comes. If all you do is hope that the future will be better you will probably still be hoping when you have one foot in the grave. You must affect changes in your life NOW! There is no other time, no other physical reality. When your goals are achieved, what day will it be? Tomorrow? Yesterday? No! At the time of their achievement it will be *today*.

Some readers may feel that this is just a play on words. It isn't. The only problem with this idea is that it is so simple that the mind has difficulty in accepting it. You were born *now*, you live *now*, and you will die *now*. In other words you live in an ever-present moment of now. Doesn't it make sense to feel that your goals have been achieved now?

You must adopt the assured attitude that your dream is already so, both mentally and emotionally. This is the principle of doing within, while you are doing without. If you think about it, when you have imagined your dreams as being already so — pretended if you like — then they really are already so in your mind and emotions. Don't look for anything hidden or complex here, this is completely straight-forward.

This attitude is, if anything, of even greater importance than being able to form clever images in your mind. Some people experience difficulty with visualisation at first. Don't worry, and don't give up. Do what you can and concentrate on feeling that your desires have already been accomplished.

You must do something

If you were to do the above and then just sit around and wait for something to happen you could be in for a long wait. Before anything will come into existence in your life you must make a commitment to doing something physical.

You are responsible for setting up the physical channels through which your dreams can be brought into tangible existence. The channel you have chosen, or are about to choose, is that of running a network marketing business. It could just as easily have been any other business, or some other form of employment, or a creative art form. But you must set up the channel. How else will you obtain the money you need?

And, of course, when the money starts to roll in, you will need to visit estate agents to look for a house, motor dealers for a car, etc. I do not wish to give the impression that these things will arrive by some supernatural means! What will happen is that ordinary events and circumstances will manifest to your advantage.

It is a good idea to begin buying small items for the new house or car you desire, or picking up brochures for that exotic holiday abroad, etc. The act of doing something related to your goal will help to ground your energy and fuel your conviction that your dreams can become real.

Be grateful for every good thing you receive

The law of gratitude is simply that abundance will flourish when the heart is grateful. When you receive the things which you have visualised and worked for, take a while to express your gratitude to life for supplying them. This could take the form of a short inner prayer or the giving of some of your money to a worthy cause.

The reason for this may not be entirely obvious at first. But if you sit back and examine how you feel when you express honest gratitude for something, you will notice that you feel relaxed. The feeling of gratitude acts as a natural antidote to tension. And tension is the killer of creative living.

Some people say that they have nothing to be grateful for. When we are going through some of life's hard times it can be hard to see the good things. But think of this: virtually every person in the industrialised world has a higher standard of health and education than even the aristocracy had a hundred years ago. We live in a degree of comfort and warmth which would have been inconceivable to our grandparents. And what about the starving masses in today's Third World? You are certainly better off than them.

When life looks bleak take a while to stand back and look sensibly at your situation. Develop a feeling of gratitude that it is not you who is hungry and suffering from malnutrition. In everyone's life there is something for which they can be grateful, even if it is only the simple gift of life itself.

You already do all of this anyway

It is important to understand that we are not talking here of doing anything which you do not do every day of your life. Everyone uses their mind and imagination to some extent, feels something about somebody or something and performs some form of activity during their day.

The problem is that usually we float about like ships which have lost their rudders. We are like flotsam and jetsam, at the mercy of any ill wind which blows our way. Many people have minds which contain so much junk of a negative nature that it is no wonder all they get is negative experiences. These people then proceed to go around bemoaning their 'bad luck'. But the only luck which exists in this world is the luck we create for ourselves.

Fear, worry and undue concern about the future, all these feelings create a mental image picture of what is *not* desired. What happens? The things we do not desire of course! Then we become enmeshed in a downward spiral of negative events breeding negative thoughts, which in turn breed further negative events, and so on . . .

But the more you control your thoughts and harness your emotions, and the more you direct your energy into purposeful activity, the more will your outer life reflect that inner attitude. What I am suggesting is nothing more or less than taking hold of the helm of your ship, in other words, your life, and steering a positive course for your own, individual, promised land.

SUCCESS CHECK

Principles of creativity:

★ everything created by man was first conceived of by mind

★ use your imagination to visualise your goals

★ feel that your goals are already accomplished

★ be grateful for everything you receive

★ take hold of the helm of your life

Feel good about yourself

Many people suffer from a poor self-image. They think of themselves as not being good enough, or clever enough, or attractive enough. But consider this: you are a unique individual, there has never been anyone like you before in the history of the universe, and there will never be anyone quite like you again. Isn't that incredible? Don't you think someone as unique and special as you ought to be feeling pretty good about themselves?

A lot of people are waiting for someone to give them permission to be happy, permission to be successful. This often stems from childhood, when we had to gain our parents' permission for everything we did. But why wait for someone else to tell you? You could wait a long time and by then it may be too late. In truth you are the only one who can give yourself the permission to be successful and happy. You have the right to expect the best in life for yourself and those you love.

Give 120 per cent commitment to living. Go on business training courses, read motivational literature, listen to motivational and self-development tapes, participate in life skills and personal growth seminars. Learn all you can about that wonderful individual which is YOU.

SUCCESS CHECK

★ **Now is the first moment of the rest of your life**

Network Marketing Success Story
CHRIS NICHOLLS
St Agnes, Cornwall

Chris Nicholls has been involved in network marketing since 1982 and is currently a distributor of For Ever Living products. Successful in two previous companies, she says she loves everything about this business.

Chris sees her responsibility when sponsoring people as that of helping them achieve whatever their individual dream may be. She has seen the business build confidence in people, has watched them flower and has flowered herself. Many friendships and long-lasting relationships have blossomed from what were initially business contacts. Network marketing has given her some of the best times of her life.

Chris is a Christian. She will not lie to anyone or dole out hype. She likes people, working with them, and believes you cannot be successful without them, no matter what business you are in. It goes without question that you have got to give good service. What matters is not so much how much you talk, as how much you *listen*. Her philosophy is that, 'people do not care how much you know, until they know how much you care'.

When she started her business, Chris made the mistake of sponsoring people who lived hundreds of miles away. She says that you have six weeks to help your people achieve some success. Ideally, you would sponsor six others with them and for them in that time. She believes that in the first few weeks and months your downlines will need your help to run their businesses. You have to do an awful lot for them at the beginning, teaching them how to teach others. But this is difficult when they live 300 miles away, and there is a limit to what you can do on the telephone. Chris strongly recommends building in your own backyard at first and leaving the long-distance work until you have built up some strong foundations and experience.

She has found women with children to be brilliant at network marketing for the simple reason that they have brought up a family. They know how to be a mother to their children, and that is basically the attitude you need to adopt towards your downlines. You need to care and nurture the people you bring into the business.

Perhaps this viewpoint explains why Chris is happiest selling health products – caring for other people's health and well-being as well as helping them to earn a good living. Her underlying philosophy is to treat other people as she would like to be treated herself – an old principle, but still valid today.

PART TWO

GETTING DOWN TO BUSINESS

8. PROSPECTING FOR GOLD

Y OUR first 90 days in this business can make or break you. It is the time when disenchantment can most easily set in. The importance of this period of time cannot be stressed too much.

You should aim to produce results quickly, and to help your downlines do the same. Growth feeds enthusiasm. When you make sales you will feel good. When you sign others into your business you will feel great. When you achieve your first goal you will feel marvellous!

SUCCESS CHECK

You have now reached the point where you have:

★ a foundation of knowledge about network marketing

★ an overall idea of what is required to be successful

★ got the paperwork together

★ set yourself a target of short, medium, and long-term goals

★ a grounding in success psychology

The most important rule you will ever learn

Ask any successful person in network marketing and they will probably tell you that the most important rule they followed is first to *make a written list of everyone you know*. Upon this list rests the success or failure of your business. I am not exaggerating. If you do not believe me, talk to a few people who have attempted to run their business without first writing a list ...

Network marketing revolves around people talking to people. If you do not have a list of such people, who are you going to talk to? Of course, there is a little more to it than simply writing down a list of names and this is what we shall study next.

But, right now, write down the names, addresses and telephone numbers of everyone you know. Don't qualify them by thinking, 'Oh, Dave would never be interested in anything like this.' The object at the moment is simply to empty your mind on to a single sheet of paper. It will surprise you to realise just how many people you know once you start making that list. You mind will be stimulated into thinking of more and more people. There may, of course, be many you do not like and would never want to work with. Put those judgements aside for the moment. You will never have to work with anyone you don't want to.

You should realise that you are not going to build your business on *who* you know, but rather *through* who you know. You should be looking to reach the people with whom your friends, colleagues and acquaintances associate. The people *you* know will lead you to the people *they* know. For instance, perhaps the postman is not interested when you tell him about your business, but he may know someone who would be and is looking for the right opportunity. Looking at it in this light, you can see the importance of including *everyone* you know.

People you can put on your list

- *Members of your own family*. Think about it. There is your mother and father; father-in-law and mother-in-law; your children; your brothers and sisters; your aunts and uncles; your nieces and nephews; your cousins; your second cousin once removed; etc.

- *Your close friends and those with whom you associate regularly*. These could be your neighbours; the people you work with; the people your spouse works with; members of your church; etc.

- *Those people you meet in organisations and clubs*. These could be civic groups; political groups; trade organisations; school organisations; sports clubs; etc.

83

- *The people you have known in the past.* Remember those old school friends you haven't seen for years; former work mates; people in towns where you used to live; old college friends; etc.

- *Those people you do business with.* This list is almost endless. They include: your doctor; solicitor; hairdresser; shopkeepers; milkman; postman; the owner of your favourite restaurant; the local rodent exterminator; etc.

- *Some lists are already available for your use.* Get out your Christmas card list; your club membership list; your list of fellow employees; your address book; etc.

Notice that your list, what is called your 'warm market', is far greater than your immediate circle of intimate friends. Literally everyone you meet during the course of your day is a prospect; either for retailing, or business building, or both.

Sorting out your list

Most people should be able to come up with a list of at least one hundred names. What you need to do now is sort them into categories, thus enabling you to determine those who are most likely to make a success of the business. These are the people you will approach first with your business proposition.

The reason this is so important is that it is difficult to work with more than five or six new people at any one time. Look at it this way. If you were to go out and sponsor one hundred people in your first month you would have a seemingly successful and fast-growing business. But what would happen to those people in the second month?

You would not have enough time to give any one person a great deal of attention. As the majority of people need a lot of help in the early stages, many would fall by the wayside. It would not be surprising to find that your downlines failed to produce anything at all.

The point to remember is, as we discussed in Chapter 4, if you work with five people, and teach those five to work with five others, and so on five levels deep – you will eventually end up with 780 people in your organisation. But you will still only be working directly with your first five. So, of course, you will see why it is unnecessary, undesirable even, to go out and sponsor everyone you come across straight away. And you will now see the importance of targeting the *best* five people you can identify from your prospect list.

The questions you must ask yourself about each prospect:

- *Are they successful in their job or business, but still seem dissatisfied in some way*? Perhaps they're not making the kind of money they would like, or maybe they yearn for greater freedom?

- *Do they have an inherent desire to be successful*? Or just a vague notion that it would be 'nice'?

- *Have they done anything in their lives which involved the possibility of failure*? Is there anything in the personality of your prospect which indicates a willingness to take risks?

- *Have they ever attempted to run their own business before*? And did they succeed?

- *Have they any previous experience of network marketing*?

- *Are they teachable*? Would they be willing to learn, or are they the know-it-all type?

- *Are they self-motivated*? People who will do nothing for themselves, and who spend half their lives hypnotised by the television, are unlikely prospects.

- *Do they own a car*? To most of us this is a twentieth-century necessity. Although it may be possible to build a small business without one, the lack of transport will make the task a lot more difficult.

- *Are they on the telephone*? The same comments apply here as to the ownership of a car.

- *Do they always seem to have more to do than hours to do it in*? These people may seem to be *too* busy. It is easy to write them off without even approaching them. But the fact is that busy people are the people who get things done. If you sell them on the idea of your business it is surprising how many will suddenly *find* the time.

- *Do they know a lot of people*? These may be either work or social contacts, but if your prospect is one of life's hermits they are going to have an uphill struggle.

● *Finally, do they have a high level of credibility amongst their friends and colleagues*? If you were presented with a business proposition from someone you distrusted, would you be interested? Of course not. Neither will anyone else.

It is now time to sift out the wheat from the chaff. Take your list and give your prospects a tick for each of the above categories for which they qualify. When you have done that you will find that some have none at all, whilst others may have all twelve. Identify the five people with the most ticks, the five with the second most ticks, etc. Rewrite your list in that order. Those with the most ticks are the first prospects to whom you will introduce your business. Those with no ticks at all should become your initial customers.

The people you are looking for are those with positive attitudes, who are willing to work for their success – not those who expect success to come looking for them. The people you want in your business are those who are eager to learn and who ask lots of questions. You do not want those who you have to continually cajole into improving their lives. Such people will drain your energy and will do little or no productive work.

It is interesting to note that those who are not going to make it will tend to resent your efforts to help as being nagging and bothersome, while the motivated and enthusiastic self-starters will appreciate your attentiveness.

SUCCESS CHECK

★ You must write down a list of everyone you know

How to obtain leads from a cold market

People are the life-blood of your business, and your prospect list is at the heart of its success. We will now look at ways in which you can continually add to that list.

Your warm market consists of the people you already have some connection with, hence they will be receptive – or warm – to you approaching them with your proposition. Occasionally you will come across someone who does not have a large warm market; others may be reluctant to 'sell to friends' as they call it; still others may want to expand more quickly than the size of their warm market will allow. It is these people who must look to the cold market for prospects.

But always remember that networking is a people-to-people business. The idea is not to go into competition with conventional direct sales forces. Tackling the cold market should only be used as a last resort. Once you have obtained a few leads from the cold market you should be aiming to get referrals from them, and hence be working a warm market again.

Continuous prospecting for new business is important because, regardless of how successful you are, you will always experience a constant throughput of people in your business. You must accept at the outset that many of the people you sponsor will not stay in the business very long. This is all part of human nature and is integral to the game you are playing. The positive side to all this coming and going of humanity is that you will occasionally come across someone like you.

Many people are tempted to work their multi-level business like a conventional business. But the methods used in traditional direct sales are not easily transferrable to network marketing. You will save yourself a lot of time, money and frustration if you take note of the following.

These are the methods of tapping into the cold market.

Leafleting

This method can work with relatively high value products. You need the value to provide the margins necessary to offset the cost of the leaflets. You will be wasting your time selling four products costing £5 each for every thousand leaflets put out, as your profit would be £10, or less; whereas four products costing £250 each, and showing a total profit of up to £500, would be a completely different matter. So, the number of MLM products for which this method is viable is extremely small. Refer back to the section on advertising in Chapter 3 — much the same comments apply here. Be extremely wary of wasting a lot of time and money.

Door-to-door canvassing

Canvassing can either be for a sale there and then, or for a later appointment. It is extremely difficult to sell anything door to door these days. Consumers simply do not like it, and they tend to distrust someone who tries this approach.

The only exceptions to this general rule are companies which produce a catalogue of everyday household consumables. The catalogue is left overnight with the customer for them to choose their purchases. It is then collected the next day, together with the order form. With the right company this can be very successful.

Telephone canvassing

This form of canvassing is an art and not everyone can do it successfully. Selling to people you don't know on the telephone is very difficult and it is not recommended for anyone contemplating network marketing. The telephone is used only to make appointments to see people to whom you have previously been referred.

Direct mail shots

Refer back to the section on leafleting. Be wary of investing in this seemingly lucrative idea, since it is not what network marketing is all about. The response rate is usually very low and you can find yourself wasting a lot of time and money.

High street interviewing

This method has the advantage of allowing you to pick your customers according to their dress and social type. It can be used successfully to find hostesses for cosmetics and jewellery parties, and for appointments to sell higher value items. It should work for most products. However, you do need a certain nerve to hang around in crowded streets waylaying people at random!

You will need to carry a clip-board with a questionnaire. The questions need to be phrased so that they lead logically to an appointment. Obviously, the questions will vary considerably from product to product, but an example is included below to illustrate the principle. The product line is a range of natural cosmetics which are not tested on animals.

N.B. Do not call this activity market research. It isn't, and you could get into trouble with the law for misrepresentation.

Sample questionnaire

1. Do you use cosmetics? Yes/No (if 'no', thank them for their time and say good-bye).

2. Do you believe that testing cosmetics on animals is good? Yes/No (if 'no' go to 3. If 'yes' go to 4).

3. Would you prefer to use cosmetics which were not tested on animals? Yes/No.

4. Would you prefer to use cosmetics which used pure, organic ingredients rather than synthetic chemicals? Yes/No.

5. Would you like to obtain your cosmetics free of charge? Yes/No (by holding a make-up party, or by joining the company and recruiting other people).

If you get a 'Yes' to any of questions 3, 4, or 5 (especially 5!), you can give your interviewee the chance to get some of her friends around for a make-up party. In addition you may be able to sign her into the business. If she doesn't want to do either you can sell her some products. The idea behind the questionnaire is to get your prospect agreeing that what you have is what she wants. When she has done this it is only a short step to doing some business.

Exhibitions

Exhibitions are those shows held in large exhibition halls such as the Ideal Home exhibition, the Boat Show, etc. Smaller shows are held throughout the year in most cities. Consult your *Yellow Pages* and choose an exhibition which will attract those people who are likely to be interested in your business/products.

You can make a few sales at these events, but your main objective should be to pick up a number of distributors. You need to be confident and experienced in handling people to follow this route. And do be wary of spending too much money. Exhibitions can cost more than the return they give.

In-store displays

Supermarkets and DIY stores are common sites for in-store displays. Unfortunately, they suffer from overkill by the double glazing companies and many people tend to ignore them as a matter of course. Not recommended.

Office and factory demonstrations

This approach works well with female-oriented consumables and fashion accessories. Be sure to obtain permission from the person responsible for the building before going in. Lunch-breaks will usually be the most convenient times.

Advertising

As far as trying to sell product is concerned, this was killed off in Chapter 3! Classified ads in newspapers can be good for recruiting, though. Try the part-time, sales and business opportunities sections. An advertisement which is short and to the point is all that is required – you do not need to spend a fortune. Your upline and parent company will advise you on wording which has been shown to work for your company and which is legally permissible, since the law on the subject is complex and often changes.

You can place your ads in:

- *Local daily newspapers.* These have a high circulation, but are expensive.

- *Local weekly newspapers.* The circulation of these is normally lower than the dailies, but they are less expensive, and you will have less competition from other advertisers.

- *Free newspapers.* These are often read by a larger number of people due to the high advertisement content. They are usually relatively inexpensive.

- *Magazines and national newspapers.* These have huge circulations and are very expensive. You need to be experienced to handle the response from these as you may get replies from hundreds of miles away. Not for the beginner.

Your objective in placing ads should be to sponsor some of the people who respond and to gain referrals from the others. When you answer the telephone, take their name straight away, then use it whenever it is appropriate. This establishes a certain informality and warmth. Your sole purpose is to convert an interested telephone call into a firm commitment to meet with you. Do not go into depth about your company and product at this stage.

Some people can feel wary of inviting strangers into their homes, especially women living alone. You can try using a public place such as hotel foyer or café for your meetings, or have a boyfriend sit in.

N.B.: There is legislation on advertising laid down by parliament (see Appendix B) by which you must abide. The law is complex and subject to change, therefore you should check with your company when considering any form of advertising, canvassing or other promotional literature. They will advise you on how to operate legally, and will also inform you of any company rules to which they want you to adhere. Ignorance of the law is no defence.

Do not pre-judge

When you put together your first prospecting list you will know the people reasonably well and will have some idea of their character. You use this knowledge to classify them into prospects for the business or for retailing.

But when you move away from people you know well, you come across a problem. How do you sort out people you do not know in any depth? Do you categorise them by profession, the size of their house, the clothes they wear? The answer to this question is, no. Do not pre-judge anyone. You must treat all your prospects equally until they sort themselves by their own actions − or lack of action. Remember, clothes do not a person make.

It cannot be emphasised enough that the whole concept of network marketing is geared towards working your warm market. Your aim must always be to create a warm market from your prospecting of the cold market. When the person you are going to see has been introduced to you via a mutual acquaintance your market has become considerably warmer. This is much more comfortable.

SUCCESS CHECK

★ Look for people who are hungry for success

Network Marketing Success Story

BOB LAMPARD
Clavering, Essex

Bob Lampard's previous business was selling public houses. He was successful, but high interest rates and other economic factors were making life tough. Bob decided to pull out before he lost money, and began looking for another way to make a living.

A friend introduced him to network marketing via a well-known perfume company. After looking into that business, Bob decided it was not for him. But he was impressed by the concept of network marketing and saw that, with the right company, he could earn a lot of money.

After investigating several schemes he eventually settled on selling Janne fashion jewellery. He felt that there was relatively little competition in this market and that he would feel comfortable with both the company and the products.

That was in October 1989. Since then he has not looked back. Bob likes the fact that, in network marketing, the ordinary man in the street can make good money. He does not consider himself to be a great entrepreneur, nor does he want to be one – but he loves the excitement of knowing he can make a sizeable income through steady and persistent effort.

Bob says that he made the mistake of spending too much money on national advertising when he first started. He feels that this is largely unproductive and can waste a great deal of time. Local advertising for distributors was much more successful, however. Because he had recently moved to the area and knew only a few people, his local contact list was small. But once he had recruited a nucleus of people he was able to expand by plugging into *their* connections. All of a sudden he found himself connected into a vast network of contacts who would pass him on to contacts of their own. Bob recommends working your warm market whenever possible. He feels that this is the most productive and efficient way of running the business.

Many of his downlines have begun by retailing the products only. Once they became proficient in this Bob introduced the concept of network marketing to them. He has found that many part-time people find the principles of multi-level retailing difficult to grasp, and so he passes them on a little at a time.

92

Bob's tips for success? Run your business as a business; and don't flit from one company to another, chasing the flavour of the month. Find a company and product range which works for you – and stick with it.

9. SHARING YOUR BUSINESS

IN contrast to the conventional, corporate world, successful network marketing people do not keep their secrets to themselves. Often, managers perceive ambitious employees as threats to their own jobs and income.

But in network marketing you benefit from those below you doing well. It is to your advantage actively to encourage those downline of you to do as you have done and consistently to turn in peak performances.

And it is this duplication – of your ability to lead, motivate and train which gives network marketing the income potential of a £250,000 franchise. Duplication gives you, the entrepreneur, greater freedom than most other occupations. You have the freedom to travel and enjoy increased leisure time, while the business you built continues to earn money for you.

But all of that is in the future. Before you can enjoy the lifestyle you need to build the business. And success or failure in this business hinges on your ability to talk to people.

Contacting the people on your list

You can do this either in person or by telephone. Both approaches have their merits and their drawbacks.

The advantages of personal contact

- You are less likely to be brushed off before you have had a chance to present your case.

- Your prospects are actually in front of you and cannot hide their body language. With experience you can get a feel of whether they are interested just by looking at them.

- You can use the appeal of your personality to much greater effect.
- You can show them the business and/or products there and then if they express interest.
- You can use visual presentation aids like leaflets and folders.
- You can demonstrate your product.

The advantages of telephone contact

- You can reach many more people much more quickly.
- You can quickly eliminate the non-starters.
- You save wear and tear on your vehicle – and on your feet!
- You save on petrol costs.
- You save time on travelling.
- Weather is seldom a problem.
- You can have prompts in front of you, and you can take notes. If you use a telerecorder you can record the entire interview and refer to it at leisure. Analysing how you handled the interview will enable you to do better next time.
- You can get straight to the point without causing offence.
- You can wear whatever you want.
- All your information is at your fingertips and can be referred to without giving the appearance of uncertainty.

Your upline will fill you in on the specific techniques which have been found to work for your particular product and company. Don't try to be clever. Your company will have developed a selling system which *works*. Deviation from this plan usually results in failure. Listen to your successful uplines and apply their advice. Below is a selection of rules which will, however, apply across the board.

- *Know your purpose.* The first point to realise is that the purpose of a telephone call, and quite often a personal visit, is not to sell your prospect on the idea of your business, but is to *set an appointment* to show your business.

● *Develop your voice*. The second point is the importance of smiling, whether you are making the approach in person, or are speaking on the telephone. With the telephone you are working with an extremely limited medium. All the other person has is the sound of your voice. When you smile you will sound more enthusiastic. And it is your enthusiasm which will transmit itself to the other person.

● *Adopt a positive attitude*. Thirdly, you must keep your mind positive and razor sharp when contacting people. It is you that the other person will see and hear. What effect will a negative, depressed attitude have on their feelings about your business? It could even be said that if you are going through a rough patch in your personal life − and you cannot detach yourself from this and get the dark clouds out of your head − you should forget about calling anyone until the inclement weather has cleared. By trying to forge ahead regardless, especially during these crucial early days, you will only frustrate yourself and lose potentially good prospects.

As has already been discussed, one of the most important factors in deciding your success or failure will be the degree of your enthusiasm. This is perhaps the single most important piece of information in this book.

You can even bungle the presentation of your product or business, forgetting half of what you were supposed to say, but if you come across as genuinely enthusiastic, a number of people will still bite. Enthusiasm is infectious.

SUCCESS CHECK

Communication:

★ know your purpose

★ develop your voice

★ adopt a positive attitude

★ be ENTHUSIASTIC!

What to say

There are a number of key phrases which will help you achieve your desired result, ie to gain an interview. Entire sales scripts could be written for you to follow, but selling is such an individual process that to formulate any rigid rules is nonsense and destroys any spontaneity. You will also find that your prospect will not have read the script. This can be extremely frustrating!

How do you react to salespeople who approach you with a patter that has obviously been fed them by their company, and which they seem to spout to every single prospect regardless? Do you find it insulting that they cannot talk to you with the respect you deserve? Most people do.

A lively, outgoing, enthusiastic personality will sell regardless of 'technique'. You should treat each of your prospects as an individual, as someone who has different priorities and goals in life to you, and to the next person you will talk to. Be genuinely interested in the other person and it will show. Be spontaneous and sincere when talking to people and you will gain their respect and their confidence.

The art is to incorporate your key selling phrases into the structure of a genuine, relaxed conversation. You must learn to lead people willingly where they want to go. Notice the phrase 'where *they* want to go'. There are selling methods that are designed to persuade people to do what the salesperson wants them to do. This may or may not be possible. It is certainly unethical. It is also bad business practice.

Whether you are retailing your product, or presenting someone with your business, you will be wasting valuable time attempting to sell to people who have no desire for your wares. If your product and business serves a valid need you will be able to find plenty of takers without resorting to such methods.

I learned this lesson many years ago when I was engaged in door-to-door canvassing. At first I tried to argue the occupier of every single house into giving me an appointment. I did not get many appointments, and I was exhausted after only a short time. Then I learned that, if a prospect did not respond positively to the initial carefully phrased questions, I was wasting my time. I thanked them courteously and went next door. I got to see many more people, with less hassle, and my appointments were solid – based on the customer's own desire, not solely on my persuasive skills.

So, here are a few phrases which you can use to gain an interview.

SUCCESS CHECK

Selling:

★ be spontaneous

★ stay relaxed and genuine

★ eliminate non-customers

'You are interested in making some extra money, aren't you?'

If they say 'yes' to this one, you are in. If they say 'no' ask if they would like more time to be with their family or indulge in their hobby; or would they like to do something more exciting for a living than making widgets in the local widget factory. If they still say 'no', forget about them as prospects for your business and tell them about the product.

'I don't have much time, so I won't keep you long'

This helps to allay any fears that you are going to sit with them all evening trying to talk them into something. Have you ever been the victim of an amateurish double-glazing salesperson, or the like? If you have you will be aware of the images people create in their minds at the first hint that someone may be about to try to sell them something. The wall they will erect between themselves and the salesperson is nothing more or less than a psychic shield. You must get right away from the stereotyped salesperson image.

This phrase is also useful for terminating an interview quickly. All you want to do is get an appointment to talk to your prospect. You should not start describing the ins and outs of your product and business over the telephone. By telling them that you are in a rush at the beginning of your approach, you will have sown seeds for a quick getaway at the end.

When using the telephone you can say, 'Hi, I was just on my way out but I thought I'd give you a quick ring before I went.' Once you have the appointment you can say something like, 'I'm sorry, but like I said, I really am in a rush. We'll go into details when I come round. 'Bye.'

'Would Tuesday or Wednesday evening be best for you?'

This is called the 'alternative choice close' and has already been discussed in Chapter 5. By keeping the time of the appointment general (afternoon, evening, etc), you are giving yourself more flexibility to fit other customers into your schedule.

'I'd like your opinion'

Everyone likes to give their opinion. Simply ask when it would be convenient to come round as you really would value their opinion of your product/business. This can be a real 'puller'.

'Would you do me a favour, I've just started this new business and I need someone to practise on?'

In the beginning this request will almost certainly be genuine! And your friends may well become interested in what you are doing.

Obtaining leads and referrals

The third-party approach

One of the most important principles of recruiting is the third-party approach. This illustrates how retailing can bring dividends in building your business as well as in moving product. Here, you do not ask your prospect directly if they are interested in making more money. The reason you don't is that the other person may feel embarrassed about admiting their need. Their response to a direct question is often a direct 'no'.

The principle can also be used after you have completed a retail sale, or when canvassing and the interviewee has said 'no' to an appointment. Do you remember the television detective, Columbo, who never solved a case until he was half-way out the door? His was an oblique approach and side-steps a lot of resistance.

As you are about to leave the person, say 'oh, by the way, I'm looking to expand my business. Do you know of anyone who may be interested in earning some extra money?'

Your prospect's response may be along the lines of, 'What is it?, or 'What does it involve?' This probably means that they are interested themselves. Or, quite often, they will say, 'Yes, me!' And they will feel that it was their idea.

Involve them in a *general* discussion about network marketing and the potential you can see in it. Whet their appetite a little. Then invite them to a meeting or a get-together over a cup of coffee to show them the details of your particular company. Do not get dragged into specifics. Say that you have another urgent appointment, but that you will tell them everything the next time you meet.

There is an important point to note here. For one-off specialities you will have to use the Columbo close on the same night as the sale. But for repeat consumables, where you will be seeing the same customers regularly each month, you have the time to build a relationship before approaching them with the business.

You can use this approach on just about everyone on your prospect list, even complete strangers. Think about the wide cross-section of people you come into contact with every day. There are people in the garage where you buy your petrol, there is your hairdresser, grocer, chemist, etc. Add a few ideas to that list yourself.

Try going up to these people and saying something like, 'Excuse me, do you mind if I ask your name?'

'Carole. Why?'

'Well, I've recently started up a new business. I wondered if you might be able to help me.'

'If I can. What is it you want?'

'I'm looking for people who are interested in earning some extra income. Do you know of anyone who may be interested?'

'Sure. I am. What is it?'

You then take her into a general discussion of network marketing, which will lead to her coming to a meeting or talking to you at a later date, etc.

Another way of using the third-party approach, suitable for people you already know, goes like this. You ask, 'I called to ask for your help. I'm expanding my business and I think you would know the type of people I'm searching for. Could you spend an hour with me? I would really value your opinion.'

By using this approach you are appealing to your prospect's

interest in giving their opinion. And any friend would be glad to help you out, wouldn't they? Of course, once they have sat down with you and seen what potential there is in network marketing, they are likely to become interested themselves. This oblique approach is especially good for business people who tend to dismiss network marketing without fully understanding what it is.

A variation on the above is, 'I know *you* haven't the time, but I think you would know people who may. Could you spend an hour ... etc.' Again, you stand the chance of interesting them in the business. But if they still remain unconvinced get to their contacts. Work the people your contacts know.

I have found that straightforward honesty can often work well. Simply say, 'Can you do me a favour? I'm looking for people to expand my business. I realise that it's not for you, but you may know someone else to whom it would appeal. I'd really appreciate your help.' Most people like to help out and will do their best for you.

The busy person

Many people, especially business people, will tell you that they've already got enough on their plate and that they couldn't find the time for another business venture.

Instead of giving up or attempting to argue them into something they don't want to do, make this suggestion: 'If you will commit two hours of your time to coming to our meeting every Wednesday − you *can* find two hours can't you? − and to supplying me with the names of your contacts, I'll do the rest.'

Show them how they can make a lot of money from those two hours a week, with virtually no work. You will work with their contacts as if they were frontline to you − you still receive commission on their sales, remember − and build your prospect's business for him. He will be at the meeting to substantiate your statements to his friends. After a short spell of this it is common for your prospect to start taking more and more interest in the business himself and you may well end up with a quality downline.

Increase your list, even when your downlines drop out!

Some of the people you bring into your business will inevitably leave. There are many reasons for this, from perhaps family difficulties and job changes to health problems. Often you will never get to fully understand the causes. Don't let this concern you. You can still rescue a great deal from apparent disaster.

When you sign up your downline you will help them to make out their prospect list. Always keep a copy for yourself. You will use this to keep track of their progress as their business builds. But, if they do pull out, you still have the list. Why not contact those people? If your relationship with your ex-downline is good − and if it isn't you have not done your job correctly − they will be happy to back you up. And don't forget, when your ex-downline's contacts come into the business they will be first level to you, which means a higher rate of commission.

Re-calling

Keep a record of those who do not sign up when you first contact them. Then get in touch every three months or so. They will be expecting you to have failed. And, as they will still be stuck with the same life problems as before, they will be likely to be more amenable to your business. This is where a subtle demonstration of your success, like showing them your new car or telling them about the holiday you are about to go on because of the business, can exert useful leverage.

Do not waste too much time on such people. Say something like, 'My business is growing fast and I don't have much time to talk'. Get a 'yes' or 'no' quickly. If the answer is 'no', leave them and go on to talk to someone else. The same principle applies to reactivating downlines who have dropped out of the business.

Do be careful that you don't waste time and energy on people who continually look for reasons why the business won't work. If you have approached them three times, and they are still negative, forget them as far as your business is concerned and move on to more productive terrain. Only continue to re-call people if you can get some sort of positive response, but something prevents them from making a commitment.

A word about professional and business people

Middle and upper income professionals can often be more open to the concept of network marketing than the average consumer, once it has been *properly explained* to them. Don't pre-judge such people by assuming they already earn all the money they could want or need. How do you know? They could be up to their ears in debt and maintenance payments; they could be earning £50,000 a year and want £100,000. Maybe they even have aspirations to become a millionaire? Or they could be deeply unhappy in their chosen career, but do not know how to find an alternative. There are many factors which could be at work in the mind of your professional prospect, not least of which may be the insecurity of modern-day corporate life.

So why not approach them with your business? You never know, it could be just what they have been looking for. But be careful, as the image of MLM may not be agreeable to some people. Some product lines may not seem to have much in the way of status attached to them. But it is surprising what a potential income of £100,000 a year can make up for ...

People will, or will not, do things for different reasons. Part of the skill of prospecting is to find your prospect's motivating desires, and then show them how your business can satisfy that desire. Start by speaking in general terms about the market for your product, the history of your company, and its growth rate. Introduce them to the concept of network marketing and how its big advantage is that there are no geographical areas to limit its growth. Show them how much money they could be earning. Do not go into specifics before you get them to a meeting. At the meeting they will talk to other successful people and absorb some of their enthusiasm. From that point on they will be starting to grasp the business and it will then be up to you to help them succeed.

The important point to remember with business and professional people is to keep your approach professional. These people are not going to be impressed by jokey amateurism. Present network marketing as a business proposition and do not dwell on the retailing of the products, as many will tend to see this as an unproductive use of their time.

The presentation

The actual presentation you give your prospect will vary from product to product and company to company. Your upline will guide you through the presentation which experience has shown to be successful. There are many variables, but it is worth mentioning a few general points at this stage.

Firstly, do not wear a suit. You will look like a salesperson and create a wall of resistance as soon as you walk in the door. Smart, clean, casual clothes are the order of the day. Remember that this is a people business. Keep your approach human — you are selling, but you are not a corporate salesperson.

Secondly, don't take up more of their time than is strictly necessary. If they miss their favourite TV programme, they will blame you for it. Also, if you take hours over your presentation they will think that they would have to do the same. Their next thought will be that they do not have the time to run a business like yours.

Lastly, be yourself. If you relax so will they. If everybody is relaxed the whole situation then becomes enjoyable. People want to do enjoyable things. They also buy largely from people they like and feel comfortable with.

SUCCESS CHECK

The presentation:

★ learn from your upline

★ do not wear a suit

★ do not waffle and waste your prospect's time

★ be yourself

Network Marketing Success Story
JIM NICHOLSON
Wotton-under-Edge, Glos.

Jim Nicholson has been in the Kleneze business since 1960. In 1969 he was at the top of the company sales league and he has stayed there ever since. By 1989, as a managing distributor, his group turnover was over £1,000,0000. And people still come up to him and say, 'Can I earn a living at this?'!

He was a London fireman when he first joined the company part time. He soon found himself making more money from selling than he was fighting fires. So, although he enjoyed his job, economics dictated that he should go full-time with Kleneze and he has never looked back. These days he puts in thirty-five to forty hours a week but stresses that in the early days, when he was building his business, he put in many more.

Jim does not believe in get-rich-quick schemes. He says that if someone offers you something for nothing, the something's for them and the nothing's for you. However, he knows many people who opt for a more modest income and have correspondingly long leisure hours in which to enjoy it. He likes the freedom which network marketing gives you to work as hard as you wish, and to work whatever hours you like.

Communication is something which Jim thinks is of great importance. To this end he produces a monthly newsletter for his downline group which he writes on his word processor. He has found this to be a good way of creating a feeling of belonging, a feeling that everyone is a part of something, and that their input matters.

Honesty counts as number one in importance with Jim. The company is honest, the products are honest and good distributors should be honest. He says that the only way to get somewhere is to work hard. He has looked at all the so-called easy ways, the gimmicky ways – but has never found a subsitute for hard work and being honest and straightforward with everybody.

10. MOTIVATING YOUR DOWNLINES

WHEN you have a job you can be idle and still get paid. But the self-employed only get paid when they work. As an employer you would have a big stick to wield over your employees. If they didn't work hard enough you could shout at them. If they turned up late you could dock their pay. As a last resort you could threaten them with the sack. Not so in network marketing. In networking the only way to get your downlines to produce more business is to motivate them. In other words you use the 'big carrot' principle.

Of course, it is true that many companies use the carrot technique as well as the stick. The more enlightened the company, the larger the carrot and the lighter the stick. The point is that in network marketing there is no stick for you to wield at all.

Your task is to learn ways in which you can influence people to *want* to work harder and more efficiently. As all your associates are self-employed and are in command of their own individual businesses, you can use no threats of any kind. What you need to develop is the art of motivation. We will now have a look at some of the aspects of this involved, and not always totally understood, psychological science.

How to be a leader

You are not responsible for the success of your downlines. But you are responsible for training them, pointing them in the right direction, and keeping their inner fire burning.

True motivation comes from within the individual, not from without. You must move something within your associates so that they will want to work hard without continually being pushed. Bear this in mind as you read this chapter. Many people make the mistake of pushing their people from the outside, when they should be giving them a gentle nudge on their inside.

The most effective technique is to combine inner and outer motivation. Outer motivation includes such devices as seminars, rallies, videotapes, etc. In other words, outer motivational input comes from outside the individual, from other people.

Inner motivation is when an unstoppable drive is ignited within a person. The desire to escape a burning building is inner motivation, for no one needs another's input to know that they want to escape the fire. Imagine then what would happen if you could find, or inspire, five people in whom the desire to succeed was as strong as the desire to escape being burned alive. You would then have an extremely successful business.

A great leader will inspire his or her followers to heights of achievement beyond which each individual previously thought themselves capable of. It is a subtle art and not easily mastered. But the further you travel along that path towards mastery, the more successful your business will become.

It is a good idea to study the lives of great leaders in all fields. It doesn't matter whether they come from military, industrial or religious backgrounds — you can learn from them all.

You need only be yourself

One of the keys to becoming a good leader is to study others who are doing well in your business. You can learn from their successes, and also from their mistakes. But do not make the mistake of trying to be the same as them.

In other words, you can improve your own ability to motivate others; but don't try to take on the personality of someone you admire. Listen to what others have to say and adapt their teachings to suit your own way of doing things.

If a technique works for you, use it. If it doesn't — even if the rest of the world seems to be succeeding with it — throw it out!

Hype versus what-to-do and how-to-do-it

At some time or other you may well go along to a 'rah-rah' motivational rally or two. When you leave one of these events you will probably, if the speakers have done their job well, be raring to go out and build the biggest network marketing business the world has ever seen.

Unfortunately, once a couple of weeks have gone by and you are stuck with the realities of everyday life, that enthusiasm has a tendency to wear a bit thin. Some people even become depressed when the hard realities of life bring them down to earth with a none too gentle bump.

The problem is usually that they have become hyped up on the rewards the business can bring — they are dreaming the big dreams and seeing themselves on that tropical island paradise counting the cheques — but no one has told them exactly what to do in order to realise those dreams, or how to go about doing it.

High-powered motivational rallies serve the purposes of showing you what can be achieved. They serve to remind you of your long-term goals. You hear successful people in your business lecture about the high rewards they have gained during their time with the company. And you will usually be able to meet them in person. Mixing with those who have already become successful will encourage your belief that you can realise your own dreams.

As such, the big rallies are useful, even vital, to your success. But never lose track of the fact that when you come home you still have a lot of hard work in front of you before those big dreams can be realised. Remember that this will apply to your downlines as well. When they come back from a rally all psyched up and ready to take on the world, make sure you give them the support of showing them *how* and *what* to do so that they will be able to see some positive results to back up the push they got from the rally.

Help your people to set goals

Not everyone is able to set goals for themselves. But everyone needs goals in order to create that sense of purpose which will be vital to their success.

Some people will want to start with small goals, such as buying some new clothes or an item for the house. Encourage them in this and work with them until they know exactly what it is they want to get out of their business. Then show them what they have to do in order to achieve it.

As time goes on, and your downlines see these small goals being realised, they will automatically upgrade their ambitions. Eventually they will come to see how they can create a lifestyle which, in the beginning, would have been impossible for them even to imagine.

Never tell people that their goals are not big enough. Try thinking of them as if they were tiny oak trees whose shoots had only just broken through the soil. With plenty of water and the correct conditions for growth those tiny shoots will eventually grow into large and powerful trees whose branches will reach for the skies. You need vision to be successful in network marketing.

The importance of weekly planning

We now come back to the subject of goal setting. You will find that people generally have difficulty in fixing weekly targets for themselves. Left to themselves, most people will do nothing. So you must help them to achieve some results.

Take the time to sit down with each of your new downlines and plan their week with them. Find out what their other commitments are and work around them. Make sure your downline brings his or her diary. When you have decided between you what the goal is for next week, ask your downline to write it down in the diary. Then they can't forget it. Ask them to write down how much retailing they are going to do, and when. And ask for a list of the people whom they will talk to about the business over the next week − then work with them day by day as they contact each person.

Do remember that it is easy to become so wrapped up in this business that all other considerations fly out of the window. But all work and no play bodes no good for anyone. Help your downlines to schedule time for their social, family and spiritual lives. Help them to maintain a balance − to work hard, but also to remember those they love.

Locate your downlines' motivating factor

Successful people became successful because they are, or once were, hungry for something. That hunger was their motivating factor.

But remember that not everyone is motivated by the thought of earning enormous amounts of money. Some people in your group will value security, while others enjoy the freedom this business can bring. As their upline you should be working with them to find out what it is that drives them to be successful, and then frequently − but subtly − reminding them of what it is they want and how they are going to achieve it.

Walk a mile in the other person's shoes

If you concentrate on helping your downlines to become successful, you will automatically become successful yourself. It is important to recognise the difference between using people and working with people. Put yourself in the position of your downline. How would you like to be treated?

Would you like to have someone breathing down your neck all the time, constantly hassling you to sell more, sponsor more, go to more meetings – all without any reference to your own desires? Or would you prefer your upline to be a person who is interested in the progress of your business, eager to help with any problems you may have, and who gives the impression of honestly wanting to help you achieve your goals, not their own?

SUCCESS CHECK

Successful motivation comes from:
★ within
★ being yourself
★ showing how to do it
★ helping your downline to set goals
★ helping your downline to plan their work
★ locating your downline's motivating factor
★ seeing life from the other person's point of view

Teach your downlines to motivate

It is not sufficient simply to motivate others. If this is all you do, you will find that your entire network will be forever dependent upon your input. That is not the idea. The idea is to create numerous independent businesses which will continue to function even if you were to go abroad for six months.

In order to reach that point you must teach your downlines how to motivate their people; and more than that you must teach them how to teach the motivating principles. When you have successfully taught five people how to motivate, and how to teach motivation, you are well on the way to that six-month holiday. We will return to this subject in Chapter 12.

110

Eventually your network will include thousands of people. Obviously, you will never be able to work with that number of people on a personal basis. Therefore, what you should be doing is identifying, and then working with, your most motivated and successful people. They, in turn, will work with another group of people, and so on. If the business is run correctly everyone should have someone close to them who they can call on for advice.

Deciding who to give time to

Do not worry about the success or failure of your downlines. It is possible to drive yourself into the ground trying to do yourself what they will not. Your aim should be to create leaders like yourself. If you do your job properly you will be sending a steady stream of confident, motivated people out into the world. They, in turn, will create people with similiar qualities to themselves.

If you find yourself getting nowhere with an individual, you need to stand back and analyse the situation. Ask yourself, have you honestly done everything possible to help that person? If your answer is 'yes', you should cut your losses and give your valuable time to someone else.

It is a strange trait of human nature that most of us will tend to give most of our time to those who do least well in the business. We tend to feel that those who are the more capable can cope by themselves, whilst those who are struggling deserve our attention. This philosophy may be true for social workers, but you are not in business to do social work. You are in business to make money.

Those who come across problems and say nothing; those who constantly need to be urged to do something; those who are always ready to throw in the towel at the slightest difficulty − these people should take up only a small amount of your time after their initial probationary period of three to four months. Remember that you only need to find five good people. When you find someone who is positive, motivated and keen to really make something of the business, doesn't it make sense to give that person your maximum attention? After all, such people are the ones who are going to produce the results.

Identifying your key people

How are you going to pick those key people with whom you are going to spend a lot of time? The short answer is that you don't − they pick

111

themselves through their activities and attitudes. Even if someone is producing little or no results, but still keeps trying, spend time with that person. On the other hand, you cannot be expected to help someone who is unwilling to help themselves.

You must train yourself to look for activity and results, and to see beyond what people say they are going to do. You are interested in what people are actually doing, not what they talk about doing. Often, the more people talk, the less they actually achieve.

Apart from the amount of sales someone produces there are several guidelines on how to recognise your potential high achievers. We discussed some likely characteristics of successful people back in Chapter 8. Now we'll look at some actions which you should look for in a serious downline.

- *A serious person will ask questions.* Those who do not ask questions are either disinterested or already know everything there is to know.

- *A serious person will bring other people to meetings.* If they are not bringing people, they are not talking to people. People who do not talk to a great many people about their business cannot succeed beyond building a small retailing operation.

- *A serious person will sit in the front two rows during your training meetings.* There is always going to be the exception, but, as a general rule of thumb, the people who arrive on time and want to get the most out of the meeting will sit near the front.

- *A serious person will take notes during your training sessions.* People who do not take notes cannot be very interested in studying the content of your meeting. Either that or they have superb memories – and how many people do you know with one of those? Again, the taking of notes indicates interest and enthusiasm.

- *A serious person will be quite happy to collect stock and other materials from your home when the need arises.* If you have to run around after other people all day you will burn too much time and energy.

Giving a nudge from below

At some point you will come across a downline who you know can do better than they are at the moment, but somehow nothing you do or say seems to have any impact. We'll call this hypothetical person Graham.

What you should do in this case is go downline from Graham and identify someone who has the potential to really go places with the business. Let's call her Sally. You build Sally up and get her business moving to the point where it is approaching, or is actually overtaking, Graham's volume.

At this point Graham should be starting to sit up and take notice, if he hasn't already. He will likely be thinking along the lines of, 'Hey, I'd better get my act together or I'm going to be surpassed by my own downline.' Hopefully, and in most cases this will in fact happen, Graham will wake up and start working.

A knock-on effect will be that Graham's figures will encourage his upline to work harder, and so on. Even you may feel this effect! Notice that Graham's motivation to work harder came from within and not from any form of outside 'rah-rah' input.

Recognising achievement

When you assign a task to someone which they have not done before, don't forget to praise them for a job well done; or if it is not so good, point out the error and praise them for their attempt. Bear in mind that if you have to criticise a task which has been incorrectly executed, never criticise the person, only their actions.

Recognition can be a greater motivator for many people than money. Everybody wants to feel good about themselves and the things they do. So use this basic human characteristic to create a feeling of worth within the person you have brought into your business. When you are talking with guests at a meeting give compliments and say positive things about your downline. Build them up in the eyes of their prospects.

People who feel good about themselves will work harder and more willingly, and for longer hours. They feel lighter and more full of energy than those who carry around a negative self-image. It takes so little to recognise another person for doing well, but it is surprising how few people apply it to their relationships. Interestingly, the giving of praise also makes the giver feel good about themselves! So it is a two-way thing.

One word of warning should be heeded before we leave this subject, however. Never, ever, give praise if you do not mean it. Not only will the recipient pick up on the fact that you are lying, but you will also

113

fall several notches in their eyes. If you lie, how will anyone ever know in the future when you are telling the truth? There will be ample opportunities for you to give genuine praise and there is no need, and no benefit to be gained, by being insincere.

SUCCESS CHECK

A successful leader:

★ *teaches* their downlines how to motivate

★ teaches their downlines *how to teach*

★ decides to whom to give time

★ identifies their key people

★ recognises achievement

Communication

Make sure you notify everyone of forthcoming meetings, rallies, guest speakers, training sessions, etc. You can also photocopy testimonial letters, magazines and newspaper articles, and anything else which you feel is of interest and value to the business. Post them to your downline leaders and ask them to do the same for their downline leaders, and so on.

Keeping in contact

It is a good idea to sit down with your key downlines regularly — ideally for at least an hour every week — to discuss their progress. Find out if they need to adjust their goals up if they are achieving them too easily; or down if they have proved to be too difficult. Never be afraid to help them to adjust their goals to accomodate the practicalities of everyday life.

The way your downlines perceive your motives for contacting them will have a tremendous bearing on the success of your business. If you give the impression that you are checking up on them you will create antagonism. Unlike the sales managers of many high-pressure direct sales outfits you cannot push your downlines into doing more business. Your only tool is your ability to motivate.

Imagine that you are ringing a downline. How will you deal with the call? If the first thing you ask them is what have they sold, what thoughts will that question generate in their mind? They will probably believe that you are only interested in how much commission you are going to make from their efforts. And they will probably be right.

Obviously, you are interested in how much commission you will receive on the sales of your downlines. It is not that you should adopt some sort of altruistic attitude here, but you should look at where you are focusing your attention.

Clear thinking makes for clear communication

When speaking to a group you will know when you are communicating powerfully and with clarity, as everyone in the room will be quiet and attentive. If they fidget and talk amongst themselves, you have not got their attention. When you speak from your heart, from the centre of yourself, you will be able to feel the focus of all those minds hanging on your every word.

Using the resources of modern technology

In this age of mass electronic communication people are able to get messages to each other at speeds which our grandfathers would have believed impossible. You can use the facilities of the microchip to enhance your network marketing business.

The advent of desk-top computers has made possible a revolution in the way small batch print-runs can be put together. This means that you can produce training material and newsletters for the benefit of your entire organisation. In the USA this has become commonplace. Some people even communicate with their downlines via cable television!

Audio and video tapes can also be useful when sponsoring people who live some distance away. After an initial telephone call send them a company video. This will reinforce what you have told them over the telephone, and will be a constant source of reference to which they can easily refer.

N.B. Do check with your company before producing any promotional material. They will have their own guidelines and they will want you to adhere to them.

115

Above all else, be enthusiastic!

Enthusiasm is the fuel of network marketing. If you are not enthusiastic yourself, how can you expect anyone downline of you to be enthusiastic? After all, they are looking to you as their model of how to run a successful business. It cannot be stated often enough that the more enthusiastic you become about your business, the more your downlines will become enthusiastic about theirs.

Like the single rotten apple in a barrel, a negative and despondent person can infect everyone else around them. Fortunately, the reverse is also true. The happy, outgoing, enthusiastic person can overcome any negative barrier. So do yourself and everyone else a favour and be enthusiastic in everything you do — be the antidote to all the negative 'can't dos' of this world.

SUCCESS CHECK

A clear communicator:

★ keeps in touch with their downline

★ develops clarity of speech

★ utilises the tools of technology

★ is ENTHUSIASTIC!

Network Marketing Success Story

DENISE HILL
Ashford, Middx

Denise Hill used to work as a ground hostess at Heathrow airport. Then a passenger asked if she was interested in earning several thousand pounds a year – part-time. No prizes for guessing her answer!

The company to which she was introduced sold natural vitamins and food supplements. She tried the products and found they helped her get through an arduous shift, feeling far less tired than before.

116

Soon it became common for travellers to comment on how fresh she looked in the early hours of the morning.

After a year in the business she qualified for a free car and found herself driving into her full-time job in a car earned from her part-time business. Something was obviously wrong with this; and it was not long before she handed in her notice at the airport.

Denise always builds depth into her downline, then, if someone drops out the other levels simply move up one rung and she doesn't lose any income. Building in depth gives her security. She also combines her network marketing activities with work as a beauty therapist, a 'touch for health' practitioner and running a slimming group. These peripheral businesses bring her into contact with a diversity of people to introduce to Nature's Sunshine products. Thus, she has ingeniously established a constant feed of new recruits to her Nature's Sunshine business.

An important tip which Denise gives is to cut down on the amount of time you spend working with non-producers. She has found that many people want the trappings of wealth, but are not prepared to work for them. They want the money, they want the lifestyle, but they are not prepared to put in the required effort to achieve their goals. She does not waste time with such people any more. She gives them three opportunities to come to her meetings. If they still don't come she will not contact them again. Denise works on the basis that if they can't get it together to come to a meeting then it is unlikely they will do anything else.

Denise has found network marketing to be the best self-development business in the world. At one time she was painfully shy, but talking in front of hundreds of people has developed her confidence considerably. She has made a lot of friends because of Nature's Sunshine, which she found difficult to do in a conventional work environment.

Finally, she leaves us with the following words of wisdom, 'The ultimate in life is finding something which you can enjoy doing, get satisfaction from, and get paid for doing ...'.

11. How to Conduct Meetings

It is vital to your success, and to that of your downlines, that everyone in your group should commit themselves to attending at least one meeting every week.

As with every aspect of your enterprise, the stronger your personal goal and the more determined you are to achieve it the greater will be the power of your meetings. It cannot be emphasised enough that you need a powerful and motivating 'reason why' to build a large and successful network marketing business.

The purpose of meetings is twofold. First, they provide the potential recruit with the chance to meet other people and to hear different points of view on the business. Second, they are occasions when your group can get together, share experiences and receive a boost of enthusiasm.

Initially, we are going to look at the different types of meeting you will come across.

The different types of meeting

Informal, small groups

These will be for up to six people, and are usually held in homes, cafés or hotel lobbies. Usually you will want to invite one or two successful associates along with two to four newcomers in order to generate lots of high-energy enthusiasm.

A small meeting has the advantage of informality, and the number of people who actually sign with your company after such an event can often be higher than that of the larger gatherings.

Keep these meetings short. Forty-five minutes is ideal, and they should never be longer than an hour. Most people's attention span will be strained at anything longer than this.

Formal company seminars

Some people refer to these as 'opportunity meetings'. However, this expression sounds a bit like the person who comes up to you and says, 'Hey, do I have a great opportunity for you?!'.

What would your reaction be to such a statement? 'Sure you do ...'. Right? In general you will do well to steer away from words such as 'opportunity'. Even the word 'meeting' can have negative connotations, creating a vision of endless boredom in many minds. You could use the words seminar, get-together, training session, conference, company briefing or marketing seminar. These expressions sound positive to the majority of people and your invitation attendance success ratio will be higher when they are used.

The larger seminars are generally held in hotel rooms accomodating twenty-five to a hundred or more people. With the increase in numbers you will find it even more difficult to keep everybody's attention, so limit your talks to forty-five minutes at the most.

After you have met a potential recruit on a one-to-one basis, or in a small group get-together, a larger seminar is the ideal next step. There, they will have the opportunity of talking to several other people involved in the business. These larger events can also inspire more one-to-one and small group gatherings. All these activities harmonise and slot in together.

A lot of energy can be generated during these meetings, and no matter how many times you have given, or listened to, the same talk, you will always find something new to learn.

The term 'meeting' is often used in this book as it is a useful and apt description of a gathering of people. The critical time to avoid its use is when you are inviting people to see your business for the first time and/or before they are committed to your company.

Rallies

Sometimes called regional training sessions or something similiar, rallies are held monthly or quarterly by your company and your top upline leaders. The numbers attending can be well into the thousands, so you can imagine how electric the atmosphere can become at times!

You, and the people you take with you, will hear the success stories of those men and women who have made it big in your business. Listening and talking to these people will help everyone to think bigger and will thus sow the seeds for future growth in your own organisation.

It is extremely important that you encourage your downlines to attend as many of these events as possible. Many people do not possess much in the way of self-motivation and will need these regular boosters to their enthusiasm to keep them going. You will find that you and your group will leave these extremely motivating gatherings with an increased conviction about the business..Meeting people who have accomplished similiar goals to you is vital for strengthening your belief in the business.

Conventions

Conventions are rallies on a grand scale and are usually held quarterly or annually. They serve the same purpose as a rally, ie motivation and training, but as they are often held in exotic locations abroad, many people combine them with a short holiday.

A word of warning should be sounded here. Don't become a convention or seminar junkie. The purpose of going to these events is to become motivated and to learn − not to latch on to some magic formula to make you rich overnight without any effort. Always remember that the purpose of everything you do in your business is to move product to the consumer. Do not get so involved in running meetings and training sessions that you forget this important fact.

Learning the skills of conducting meetings

It is possible to run a successful business just by using the meetings which other people set up. However, you will be at the mercy of last-minute cancellations and changes. Running your own meetings will give you increased control over your business.

Of course, no one would expect you to jump straight into organising a conference for a thousand people! Take it at a steady pace. Begin with informal gatherings of half a dozen or so and when you feel confident, and the size of your business justifies it, look into putting on your own show, perhaps at a local hotel.

The best way to learn about organising meetings is simply to help your upline put one on. By being at the meeting, acting and speaking positively, bringing others and sharing your experience of the business, you will become an asset your upline will think worthy of investing time with. At some point during the evening introduce your own prospects to your upline and other successful people. Maintain a high profile. Circulate.

The hotel room used for any large gathering incurs costs both in terms of money and in energy expenditure. Your volunteering to help with the setting up of equipment, welcoming people at the door and then clearing up at the end of the session will be gratefully received by the organiser.

Consider what will happen when you become active in your upline's meetings:

- you will become more enthusiastic about your own business;
- you will become more knowledgeable about your business;
- it will be easier for you to invite people because you are always attending yourself;
- you will establish greater credibility with your downlines and prospective recruits when they see you are actively involved.

Be aware of the fact that all the time you are helping your upline with their events that this is a training process for you. Look, listen and learn. Observe and make notes. Become a sponge and absorb knowledge, as you will soon be applying the same principles of success to running your own independent seminars.

When you feel you are ready to stretch your own wings, have a word with your upline and schedule a few dates. For the first two or three you may like to have your upline around, in case you run into unforeseen difficulties. But once you have gained a little experience you will find your confidence increasing in leaps and bounds.

Learn how to invite

If your prospect is a stranger say, 'You don't know me, so I'd like to take you to meet some others.' But if it is someone you see often say, 'You know me, so I'd like you to meet some others.' With the deletion or addition of 'don't', this one phrase can be used to invite everyone you meet!

Another good line is, 'Just give me half an hour.' Most people can spare that amount of time and, once hooked, they will probably stay longer.

To get people actually to arrive at your meeting why not pick them up yourself? It is an undisputed fact that 100 per cent of the people you take to a meeting yourself will actually arrive! But the success rate

121

can be somewhat lower if you leave them to their own devices.

Get the people you invite to make a positive commitment. Ask them to check their diaries and make a note of the date. If you say that you need to know for sure that they are coming because you are only inviting a few people, it will make the meeting sound more exclusive. Most people will feel flattered and will be more likely to arrive. If they say they are going to try to make it, they are politely telling you that they have no intention whatsoever of being there.

If you can get your guest to bring a friend along that will deepen their commitment. That friend will also help in counteracting any negative influences your prospect may meet up with on their return from the meeting.

It is also a good idea to give your prospect a motivational audio or videotape when they leave the meeting. Again, this will help to offset any negative opinions they may get from people who were not at the meeting and who know nothing about the business.

Avoiding negative questions from your audience

Network marketing, as we have already discussed, is a widely misunderstood concept. That being the case, you are likely to attract the occasional person to your meetings who is ignorant of the facts and is antagonistic to the idea. If these people are allowed to voice their opinions in public it can sour the attitude of everyone else in the room. This is the 'rotten apple' principle at work again.

You need to find a way to keep these people quiet until you have a chance to explain the realities of multi-level life to the group as a whole. Fortunately, this task can be easily accomplished.

Your presentation of your company's business plan should be formulated so that it answers the majority of frequently asked questions before they are asked. Explain this to your audience, then ask them to refrain from asking questions until the end of your talk. Tell them that all the facts will be presented to them in a logical and easily understood order. Anyone who ignores such a reasonable request will get no sympathy from the rest of the audience, and you can safely ask them to sit down and wait until the end.

When you have finished your presentation, ask everyone to get back together with the person who brought them to the meeting, so that they can answer any unresolved questions. Thus, everyone is satisfied, and the negative types get no chance to spoil things for the others.

122

There are basic questions which come up time and time again. Your talk should cover all of these. They are as follows.

- The name and history of the company. Is it financially sound? What is its growth rate, credit rating, etc?
- Is your product or service needed?
- Is it priced correctly? Essentially, is it something they could sell in today's market-place?
- What is the commission schedule? How much money can they make?
- What will be the extent of their financial commitment?
- What are the advantages of network marketing over conventional business and employment?
- How is the business operated? What will they have to do?
- How much of their time will it take up?

During your introductory remarks you should tell your audience about the main areas you will be dealing with. Thus, you will have primed them to accept and listen to the bulk of your talk.

The main part of your presentation will cover the subjects you mentioned in your introduction but in greater depth, and your summing up will state again what the evening has been about. There is no substitute for the old gospel teacher's maxim, 'First, ah tells 'em what ah'm goin' to tell 'em. Then ah tells 'em. Then ah tells 'em what ah told 'em'!

Keep your talk to general terms only. Most people will not absorb detail. Use stories and analogies to create interest and hold their attention.

Keep your meetings simple and it will then be easy for others to duplicate them. Flashy presentations may get you a pat on the back but they will deter other, less confident, people from having a go. Remember that everything you do must be able to be duplicated by the average person.

On the door

The first impression that your prospect has when they enter the meeting room is vitally important. Always have someone on the door to welcome people. Have them say something along the lines of, 'I'm glad you were able to make it this evening. Enjoy the presentation. If you have any questions come to see me after the seminar and either I or someone else will do our best to answer them for you.' This will

123

create a warm feeling towards your business and will set people at ease. If they are not with someone you know, make sure you take their name, address and telephone number so you can contact them after the meeting.

Start punctually

You must present a professional image. The punctual keeping of appointments is indicative of a basic courtesy and respect when dealing with people on a one-to-one basis; so why should things be any different when keeping an appointment with several people?

Seating arrangements

You should set up 50 per cent fewer chairs than the number of people you expect to be attending. A roomful of empty chairs creates the impression that your meeting has not been as successful as you anticipated. But, having to get out extra chairs to meet the demand creates a feeling of excitement because it appears that even more people than you expected have shown up.

Smoking

Don't. Smoking is only socially acceptable these days in pubs and, becoming less so, in restaurants. Most smokers today realise that they need to restrain themselves when in company and you will find few problems if you erect a 'No Smoking — Please' sign.

Refreshments

If your meeting is in a hotel there should be no problem since your guests can make use of the hotel facilities. When holding a small meeting in your home do remember to keep any cakes, etc, simple. You do not want to put people off your business just because they feel they cannot match your cordon bleu standards. For this reason, there is something to be said for buying all your edibles at the local supermarket.

Drinks should be non-alcoholic if the gathering is in your home. No one will be offended if you do not serve alcoholic beverages, but someone might be if you do.

Products and brochures

Always have a selection of your products on display at the front of the room. Refer to and demonstrate some of them during your presentation. Leave plenty of brochures scattered around so that your guests have something to pick up and read.

Children

Love them we might, but keep them out of the way when presenting your business. They can be distracting and give the appearance of amateurism.

Signing up

Always have application forms and starter kits on display so that anybody who wants to can sign with your company during the meeting, but don't push this. Apart from the ethics of hyping people into joining your business, many people will be turned off by the faintest whiff of high-pressure techniques.

Follow up

You should always be in a position to offer enquirers follow-up meetings and training sessions. This ensures continuity and will bolster their enthusiasm while they are digesting the information you are presenting them with. Take your prospect's business card and telephone number. If you wait for them to call you, you could be in for a long wait.

When you do call, ask some of the following questions.

- Can you see yourself setting up in business with this company?
- How would you like to approach the business?
- Would you like to be full or part-time in three months' time?
- When would be a convenient time to go through the paperwork and get you started? Would tomorrow afternoon or evening be best for you?

During the delicate period between your prospect being introduced to your business and making a commitment by signing up, keep in constant contact. Their enthusiasm can go off the boil rapidly, when you are not there to support it. Your objective should be to get them working as soon as possible.

SUCCESS CHECK

Conducting meetings:

★ commit to at least one meeting every week

★ participate in organising your upline's meetings

★ invite people to every meeting

★ first impressions count; welcome people at the door

★ find a babysitter for your children

★ start punctually

★ answer all standard questions in your talk

★ set out 50 per cent fewer seats than the total number of people expected

★ do not smoke

★ keep refreshments simple

★ display products and brochures

★ have application forms and starter kits ready

★ follow up after the meeting

Training sessions

A comprehensive training schedule is crucial to the success of your business. Practical field training will be the single most important element in your programme. Reinforce this with theoretical classroom work.

You will find that the more you share your knowledge and experience with others, so, in turn, your own wisdom will grow. When you sign up a new person you should take them out with you on retailing and sponsoring presentations as soon as possible. You must get them trained and moving quickly. Unless they see some results fast they will soon lose enthusiasm for the business.

Show your downlines how to run their business by letting them watch you run yours. This will increase their confidence in you as a person and in what you are telling them about the business. It is no use just telling people what to do. You must take them by the hand and actually show them.

A fast-growing business will require training seminars every week to cope with the influx of new people. They should cover all aspects of your business from retailing and product knowledge, to building a network. Evenings and weekends are usually best for most people, or it means them having to take time away from their present employment. This will be a negative factor for some people, and you need to make life as easy as possible for new recruits to your business.

In the early stages you can use your home, but, unless you are fortunate enough to own a house with a suitable-sized room, you will soon need to move out into a hotel or office location. Cost will now become a factor and sharing the expense with others should help.

For a business seminar it is important that everyone dresses appropriately. A newcomer entering a room full of people lounging around in dirty jeans and sweat shirts is not going to be impressed by the professionalism of the company. The clothes we wear reflect our inner attitude, and our inner attitude is affected by the clothes we wear. Personal hygiene works in a similiar manner. Bear this point in mind; it is important. Remember that you are running a business.

For a training session it is not necessary to be so strict. The wearing of jeans is not recommended but for an intensive all-day training session it is important for people to be as relaxed as possible. If wearing a suit relaxes you, fine. Wear it. But if you feel a certain restrictiveness about such clothing, why not wear something more comfortable?

Listen to each other

It is good for both you and your downlines to hear views on the business from other people. Quite often you will find that a point you have been trying to get across to someone for weeks, will become clear to them in seconds when it is explained by someone else. Do not take this as a slight on your teaching skills, it is simply a fact of human nature. The mind sometimes erects subconscious blocks to learning, but when approached from a new angle the information suddenly gets through. This can be particularly important when you are emotionally close to the person you are instructing, which is also why driving and flying lessons are best left to strangers.

Using modern technology

Most people will forget most of what is said during the best-planned training session. That is human nature. But there is no need to accept that situation.

As we mentioned in Chapter 10, microelectronic technology offers a host of portable recording equipment which can be used to enhance your business. Audiotaping is the simplest of course. Encourage the taping of training sessions and business seminars. Your downlines will be able to replay the whole session over and over again whilst they are driving, or, with a portable cassette player, doing household chores. Constant repetition will gradually cement the principles of the training into their minds so that they will never be forgotten.

Video cameras have now become an affordable item for most people. Why not use one to record your training sessions and business seminars? As with audiotapes you will find it valuable to be able to hand out recordings of a training session which your downlines can watch over and over again. At the very least you will obtain some interesting feedback on how you come across to people, and, if the film looks professional enough, you can give it to enquirers into your business.

Videos are frequently used in industry to evaluate performance in interview situations and as a training aid when instructing people about public speaking. There is no reason why you cannot do the same. As long as you and your downlines are willing to face up to the sometimes ego-deflating experience of watching yourselves perform you will become powerful and persuasive speakers. And the growth of your business will reflect this.

Other useful equipment includes dry-wipe boards, overhead projectors and slide projectors. Without these items your ability to communicate with a large audience may be seriously restricted.

All of this may sound costly. But don't worry, you don't need to spend a great deal of money until your business is producing enough money to cover the expense ten times over. Again, sharing the load with your downlines and upline leaders will reduce your own financial input. Always remember that this is a team business.

You will find everyone goes away encouraged and determined to increase their efforts after a good training get together. Keep them fun and people will want to return.

```
┌─────────────────────────────────────────────────────────────┐
│                                                               │
│                     SUCCESS CHECK                             │
│                                                               │
│   Training:                                                   │
│                                                               │
│   ★ people need to see results quickly                        │
│                                                               │
│   ★ let your downlines watch and learn from you               │
│                                                               │
│   ★ run training sessions each week                           │
│                                                               │
│   ★ dress smartly but comfortably                             │
│                                                               │
│   ★ listen to the points which each person brings up          │
│                                                               │
│   ★ use technological aids                                    │
│                                                               │
└─────────────────────────────────────────────────────────────┘
```

Not all meetings need to be business meetings

It is only natural that people want to enjoy the means by which they earn their living. It is also natural to desire to know more about the people with whom you are working.

Life consists of a lot more than just earning money. Your downlines will be more likely to stay in your business if they feel you care about them as people and not only about the amount of sales they are producing. One way to foster this feeling is to put on social events to which they, and their spouses and friends, are invited.

Parties, barbeques and camp-outs are obvious examples of the types of events you could put on. Not so obvious perhaps is the way in which fun activities can be combined with business meetings. A combination which has been proven to work well is that of paint-gun games in the morning, a business get-together in the afternoon, followed by a rave-up party in the evening hours.

Conversations will inevitably centre around the subject of network marketing and if you allow your downlines to bring friends along there will almost certainly be an upsurge in the size of your business over the following weeks. An enjoyable weekend away from the tedium of everyday life can work wonders for the morale of your whole organisation. Even those who do not participate will feel the effect of the other's enthusiasm.

The costs of such an exercise can be recovered by charging for tickets. Once word gets around that these events are not only great fun but tremendously helpful to building a successful business, you will have no shortage of takers.

SUCCESS CHECK

★ **Keep it fun!**

Network Marketing Success Story
DAVE AND PAT McCUNE
Comber, County Down, Northern Ireland

Dave and Pat McCune first went to an Amway meeting simply to keep a colleague quiet. To their surprise the meeting was interesting and they were impressed by what they saw and heard. They took it from there and Amway became their full-time business in 1981.

At the time of their introduction to network marketing Dave was working as a computer operations controller and as a semi-professional musician. He had reached as far as he was going to go in his corporation and was looking for a new challenge, especially if it was something in which he could be independent. He liked the flexibility inherent in the networking concept. He saw that he would be working with a team, but without losing his individuality. And the fact that there are no territories, unions or employees to worry about confirmed that Amway was to be his and Pat's way forward.

They have come to love the business so much that they never count the number of hours they put in – as we do not count the hours we give to any enjoyable activity or hobby. Dave plays his music purely for the love of it now, as his Amway business provides the freedom to pick and choose the gigs at which he plays. Before, he had to take whatever he was offered just to earn some money.

They place great value on loyalty. Dave says that people who switch companies regularly, going for the promise of higher rewards like some MLM junkie, will never develop solid businesses. He feels that if they are not loyal to their company they are unlikely to be loyal to their downlines either.

130

The McCunes' adhere to the philosophy that 'people move products – products do not move people'. They believe that many people go wrong by placing the emphasis on the product. In network marketing the emphasis should be on people, creating friendships and a family-type atmosphere. This builds strong foundations. They point out that it is one thing to build a large income, but it is quite another to keep it together. If the foundations are weak (built on product, not people) your network will peak, and then collapse underneath you.

One mistake which they often see people making is that of going to unqualified people for advice. The local butcher or the next-door neighbour is unlikely to be experienced in network marketing! And nine times out of ten their 'advice' will be negative anyway. So, do find people who have gained some real experience and listen to them instead.

Dave and Pat never stop learning about networking. They say that the day you stop learning is the day your business dies. After all, how much do we know about ourselves? Probably not a lot. So it follows that we don't know a great deal about other people and how they operate either. There is always something new we can learn about ourselves and others, and, as this business is all about people, there is always something new we can learn about network marketing. Dave's final quote is this, 'Keep growing, keep learning, and keep setting new goals.'

12. HOW TO BUILD YOUR BUSINESS

IN the next two chapters we'll be looking at a host of techniques which have been proved to work in the maelstrom of everyday life. They represent the hard-won knowledge of hundreds of successful men and women – the distilled experience of many years in the market-place.

After a certain point is reached your business will begin to 'take off'. This is where you start to reap the rewards of all the hard work you put in at the beginning. You will then see your income growing without any noticeable extra effort on your part. This is because the people you have trained and put out into the world as your downlines are now producing significant business. Not only that, but they are training downlines of their own, who are themselves producing sales, etc . . .

If it could be said of your first days in business that you did more than what you got paid for, now it will feel as if you are being paid for more than you do. The attitude you need to adopt is that of the marathon runner, not the sprinter.

SUCCESS CHECK

★ Success requires stamina

The only people who lose are those who quit

So many people give up in any field of endeavour when they are, unbeknown to them, close to success. You've probably heard the story of the miner who spent half his life in search of gold, only to quit in defeat. The guy he sold out to dug six inches into the rock face and struck a rich vein of the precious metal. You don't want to give up when you are six inches from success, do you?

An example from my own life illustrates this same point of going the extra mile. A few years ago I spent some time in Israel. At that time the Sinai desert was under Israeli control and it was common to travel down the coast in search of a Red Sea paradise.

My travelling companion and I had heard many stories of the wonderful beaches and coves to be found at the southernmost tip of the Sinai peninsular in a place called Sharm-el-Sheikh. So, loaded with provisions, we boarded a bus and headed south. We arrived in Sharm at two o'clock in the morning and were unceremoniously dumped. We spent the night in sleeping bags on the open beach.

The blistering morning sun brought us confusion and disappointment. We saw that we were in a large bay. The beach was of unenticing pebbles strewn with twentieth-century debris. Behind us was the distinctly frontier town of Sharm. To our right was an army garrison. To our left was a rugged promontory. Not exactly a paradise!

Twenty others had been left stranded on the same beach with us. All of us were confused, and many were muttering that they had been conned and lied to about the beauty to be found in this apparently desolate place. I saw several get on the first bus out. The only possibility seemed to be that something must be lying around that rocky promontory.

It looked easy, standing on the beach, but when I started to explore, the terrain became rougher and rougher. I was not the only one who had the idea of trying that route, but gradually our numbers thinned out as the others turned back — disillusioned that something which looked so easy presented obstacles they had not bargained for. The promontory constantly gave rise to the hope that over the next rise, or round the next corner, would be the dream I had been seeking. Each time the promise was proved to be false; all there was was yet another hill to climb.

I, too, was close to being beaten when I faced yet another boulder-strewn incline. I was tempted to turn back there and then, but something urged me to make one last effort. If that came to nothing, I thought, I would turn back.

As I reached the top of that slope a magnificent panorama of a small, gently curving cove, golden sand and rich, blue water hit me between the eyes. My companion and I spent two weeks living on that wonderful beach, and I shall never forget how I nearly gave up the search when I was only a few feet from my goal.

SUCCESS CHECK

★ **Go the extra mile!**

You can't lose what you have never had

Do you remember those discos we went to as teenagers? They were packed with young men and women all eager to find someone of the opposite sex. But how many ended up going home alone?

The guys who talked to half a dozen or more girls in an evening always stood good odds of going home with one of them. Like selling, chatting up the opposite sex is a numbers game. Many of you may be shy of approaching someone with your products or business plan. But think about it. What have you to lose?

The person you have your eye on is not a customer or associate of yours at the moment, and if you do not talk to them they will certainly never become one. If you do offer them the chance either to buy or sell your products, at least there is the possibility that they will say that word so beloved by all in sales − 'yes'.

SUCCESS CHECK

★ **You have nothing to lose except your inhibitions**

Some will, some won't − so what?

Some people will buy your products and some will not. This is a fact of economic life. You will feel elated when you sell, and maybe a little bit down when you do not.

Likewise with sponsoring. Some will want to join with you in your business, others will not. Some will be successful, others will not. All this is perfectly natural. Some people are going to say 'no' to you. Some people are not going to achieve the results you were hoping for them. Do not take it personally. Selling is a numbers game.

A way of keeping things in perspective is to think of it like this. For the sake of argument, let's assume you have a speciality product on which you make a profit of £60, and that your conversion rate of presentations to sales is one in three. On average, for every three presentations you make you will earn a profit of £60. So if you look upon each rejection as being worth £20 you can cheerfully wave goodbye to each prospect knowing that you have just made £20.

A relaxed attitude will increase your sales. How do you feel if a salesperson comes across to you as being desperate to make a sale? You think, why is this person so desperate to sell this product? What's wrong with it? But a casual take-it-or-leave-it approach implies confidence that the salesperson can easily sell to someone else, even if you don't buy. You should adopt the same attitude if you are handling a catalogue of consumables or are talking to people about your business.

Detachment is the name of the game. If you are going to curl up in agonies of personal rejection every time you don't make a sale or fail to sign someone up, you are in for a tough ride. So what if the last person said, 'no' – the next one is going to say, 'yes'!

A word about salespeople

This is a selling business. It is a strange paradox, then, that many professional salespeople fail in network marketing. As you will come across many salespeople – you may even be one yourself – it is important for you to understand the difficulties they will face.

But let's get one thing clear at the outset. It is not that salespeople are no good for this business. They can be brilliant – if they work the business in the correct manner. Unfortunately, many salespeople think they know all there is to know about selling and refuse to listen to advice.

The problem is that network marketing is much more of a teaching business than a selling business. Sure, you are exchanging goods for money, which is selling by anyone's definition of the word. But the successful people spend the majority of their time teaching others how to build their businesses. Their retail sales occur as part of a total marketing strategy − they are not the only goal they focus on.

TTT − Teaching Tony to Teach

Let's say you've sponsored a top-line salesman. We'll call him Tony. If his reaction is like that of most salesmen Tony will immediately see the business as revolving around personally retailing a lot of product. He is a professional salesman; he can put his own presentation together; he can work with strangers, no problem − just keep out of his way and he'll sell like crazy!

'Sounds good', you say. After all, that's what you need to do isn't it − sell product? Well, the answer is yes, and no. It is true that some people will be content to make a part-time income from simply retailing the products. That's fine, but a professional salesmen will soon find that the profit potential of most MLM goods is not great enough to justify the amount of time he's spending on the business. He will soon realise that he would be financially better off selling kitchens or some other high-value, high-profit product. For example, one £6,000 kitchen would net him £600. No multi-level product can match that degree of profit from just the one sale.

So you explain to Tony that he must sponsor other people into his business in order to make the big money he is interested in. You explain to him that he should look upon retailing as a way of prospecting for new downlines, and not just as a selling opportunity. That way the return from his time invested in the business will be increased dramatically. You show him how one good new associate could be worth countless kitchen sales to him.

But what does Tony do? He goes off and tries to sponsor the whole world! Soon he has over a hundred people in his organisation. Over a hundred people frontline to him. No one can possibly handle that number of people and soon the inevitable happens. They start falling away from the business. Tony has not had time to teach them how to run their business, and if they are not adequately taught 99 per cent of people will fail.

The scene is now set for disaster. Tony's downlines are dropping out as fast as he can recruit new people. They are also not producing anything, since Tony has not taught them how to produce. It will not be long before Tony tires of this state of affairs − he still thinks he could be making more money selling kitchens − and, believing the whole business is a con, goes off to find something else to sell. His downlines see him pack in the business and they disappear with him. You, seeing Tony fail and not make you rich the way you had hoped, also become discouraged and before long you are also looking for something else.

This sad state of affairs is not an exaggeration. It is a fact that the scenario illustrated above happens every day of the week. But, with the application of a few simple rules, the whole disaster could have been averted. It all revolves around finding people who are teachable. If you can find a salesperson who is willing to listen to you and learn a radical new approach to marketing, they could be worth a fortune. Unfortunately, all too many of them are not willing to listen and learn. Generally, you will be better off recruiting five teachers rather than five salespeople.

SUCCESS CHECK

★ **Find people who are willing to learn**

You must sponsor at least three levels deep

If you only sponsor to one level, and do not teach that level how to sponsor, what will happen? First, all they can do effectively is retail the product − that's what Tony tried. Secondly, if you move away or go abroad your business will collapse, because no one knows how to operate without you being there in person to help them.

But if you teach your first level, we'll call her Sandy, to sponsor her friend Gerald, your business is now three levels deep. When you have taught Sandy how to sponsor, she can keep doing that even when you are hundreds of miles away.

Ah! I hear some of you thinking, so that's the secret of network marketing, right? Wrong. At this point Sandy is like Tony. She has learned to bring others into the business, but she is still lacking one vital ingredient. She does not yet know that she must teach others.

You must teach Sandy how to teach Gerald to run his business. She must teach him how to teach someone else how to sponsor − and how to teach others how to sponsor. And so this process becomes self-replicating. It all depends on your ability to teach others to do what you do.

This is how the freedom of network marketing comes about. If you can set up as little as five good people who will teach others to teach, the opportunity is there to be able to relax for six months of the year.

SUCCESS CHECK

★ **You must learn to teach others how to teach**

Build your business with depth as well as width

Although the commission structure of individual companies will vary, certain principles are common to most. One of these is that the people who are personally sponsored by you − often called your frontline − usually earn you more than those who are four or five levels deep. Therefore, the greater the number of people you have in this position, the more quickly will your income grow. This is the aspect of the business that Tony latched on to in our earlier example.

Width is a good thing. You should only work with five new people at a time, yes; but when they are trained and capable of fleeing the nest, you let them go and find others to take their place. Eventually you could end up with scores of people frontline to you, but you only work with five new people at a time. The importance of this point cannot be overemphasised.

If you receive commission on only your first five levels, some of you may wonder why you should need to consider building further than this. But what would happen if your business was only built to five levels and one level dropped out? You could lose a lot of money. But if you had built to six levels deep, everyone would simply move up a rung. So your income would remain stable. Most of us value a stable income as well as high growth potential, so this factor is worth keeping in mind.

Depth is a measure of how well you have trained your downlines to teach others to teach. Depth gives you security. If your business has grown seven, eight, or more levels deep, losing a few people now and again will have little effect on your income.

It is common for successful people to work with downlines so deep in their business that they will not immediately receive any income

138

from their efforts. It requires a powerful vision to be able to do this, but the end results can be explosive.

Once a certain point is reached in a network business, a chain reaction is set into operation. The principle is similiar to nuclear fission in that every particle collides to create two more new particles, which then also collide, creating another four new particles, and so on. Once a certain level of energy is reached this chain reaction becomes virtually unstoppable. If you build your business to this point you will find it continuing regardless of whether you are involved or not. If you create enough self-motivated teachers you will not be able to prevent them from earning you extremely large amounts of money.

SUCCESS CHECK

★ Depth gives you security

★ Width gives you high commission

Network Marketing Success Story

SHARON COX
Polegate, East Sussex

Sharon Cox started in the Kleneze business when her youngest child was only six weeks old. She put the carry cot and a few bottles on the back seat of her car and off she went. At first she viewed the business simply as a way of topping up the family household budget. But when it took off she began to take a more serious look.

Being a busy mum and wife, she likes the flexibility of network marketing. She finds that she can gear the business around her life, instead of having to gear her life around a business. If she chooses not to go out one day she can catch up the next. She still takes her children with her, giving them a half-hour break to play on the swings when they become bored.

Sharon has found that many people like the fact that you do not have to be a salesperson to be successful. She builds her business simply by mentioning it to friends and by a small amount of local advertising. Whenever she is in contact with customers or agents, Sharon makes sure she acts and speaks positively. Smiling when speaking on the telephone has proved to be especially valuable. But she has noticed that when she slacks off, so does her group. So she takes care always to lead from the front, following the policy of not asking anyone to do anything which she does not do herself.

One of Sharon's prime motivating factors is that the more she puts into her business, the more she gets out. Whereas, in most jobs, no matter how hard you work you still only receive the same wage as the next person. Her final comment was this: 'What other business can you start in with no money and no experience, and be in profit from day one?'

13. HOW TO WORK YOUR BUSINESS

It is a fact of network marketing life that 80 per cent of sales are produced by 20 per cent of the sales force. Ask yourself with whom will your time be most profitably spent — the unproductive 80 per cent or the high-flying 20 per cent?

The first reaction of many people is to try to get the majority to do what the minority is doing. After all, they're the ones who need help aren't they? Theoretically, yes; but in practice you will be wasting your time.

Think of it like this. Imagine you are growing a crop of vegetables, say carrots. When the seedlings have reached a certain stage in their growth, you select the strong and discard the weak. Then you give the strong ones all the care and nourishment they need in order to grow into large, healthy carrots. You would not spend all your time looking after the weak seedlings would you? The same principle also applies to the people you bring into your business.

If you spend your time with the people who show a real potential for growth, your own business will grow. If you spend your time trying to help those who will not help themselves you will exhaust yourself, and you will look back on your business in six months and wonder why it isn't going anywhere.

SUCCESS CHECK

★ Spend your time helping those who help themselves

Finding the time

We all have only a certain, finite, amount of time to devote to our business. Even if network marketing was your sole occupation you would still only have twenty-four hours a day to give to it. Time is a valuable commodity. How we use it is of the utmost importance.

How are you going to decide what to do today? Maybe you have recently signed with a network marketing company and you are working yourself up to actually doing something with your business. Have you ever told yourself that you'll start after you've taken the dog for a walk – then come home only to realise that you haven't read the paper yet. You sit down with the gossip for an hour or so and then notice that there is an interesting documentary on the television. This takes you up to bedtime and you go to sleep determined that tomorrow will be different, that you will try to begin your business then.

Of course, tomorrow is never different. There is always some way to justify not starting your business. After a few weeks of this many people become disenchanted with network marketing, swearing that it doesn't work. If you could take a peep into their homes you would probably see their starter pack sitting, unopened, on top of the television.

It is not so much the amount of time you have available which counts, but what you do with it. You can while away your alloted hours indulging in passive entertainments, achieving little or nothing. Or you can work smart. As you have already had the gumption to pick up this book you are probably halfway there already; so let's look at some ways in which you can maximise the use of your time.

Eliminate, or reduce, the amount of time you spend watching television

Don't misinterpret this and believe that you should become anti-TV. It is simply a question of priorities. What do you want to do most: realise your dreams – or live in someone else's dream?

Try adding up the time you spend in front of that hypnotic, glowing tube. Then make your choice.

Do your most important tasks first

It is no use fixing the roof of your home if the foundations are sinking in quicksand! Always do the most pressing, urgent jobs first. If you follow this rule you will find that everything gets done in an orderly and sane fashion. When you are first starting up your business you will need all the time and energy you can find. So, put aside all non-critical household tasks in favour of selling product and sponsoring others.

Apply the following criteria to all household and business pressures: if it is not done, will anyone be in danger or will they suffer in any way? And will your world collapse if the task in question is left until tomorrow? If you draw a negative on both counts, forget the task and work your business instead.

Keep a things-to-do list

You may first realise the value of lists when you come back from shopping expeditions having achieved only half of what you set out to do. This is not only frustrating, but is also an incredible waste of time.

The same principle applies to business activities. Make a list of what needs to be done − in order of importance − and work your way through it, starting at the top. When you look back in three months time you will be staggered to see how much more you have achieved; and you will probably be using less energy than it previously took you to do half as much.

SUCCESS CHECK

Organising your time:

★ reduce the time you spend watching television

★ do the most important tasks first

★ keep a things-to-do list

Spend 90 per cent of your time on new business

You are in business to move your products from the manufacturer to an end consumer. Your success depends on finding ways to increase the quantity of product you distribute. Therefore, you should always be prospecting for new business.

Opportunities abound, even when you are seemingly committed to working with existing associates. Supposing you were on your way to a company meeting? Who could you approach with the business?

There is the taxi driver who takes you from the railway station to the hotel or airport. What about the receptionist? Waiters and waitresses? The hotel manager? The person who sells you a newspaper to read on the train? The passengers you sit next to? Some people may not have the nerve to approach strangers in this way, but just think what you may be losing out on. The lady vaccuuming the hotel foyer could be a dissatisfied successful just waiting to hear about your business. Don't turn your nose up at anyone. Many, many successful people in network marketing have little or no formal qualifications.

People will come and go in your business. That is a fact of life. Therefore, you need to be constantly recruiting to fill their places. Out of every fifty people you bring into the business you can reckon on one or two doing something really serious with it. And in order to bring in fifty you need to have talked to at least three times as many. So don't pre-judge anyone. You never know, inside that cleaning lady there may be a millionaire trying to find her way out.

This is a cash business

Your parent company will not release product until it is paid for. This means that there will never be a problem of bad debts for them. Neither should there be for you. I strongly recommend that you do not hand over anything without first receiving payment in full. You should apply this rule to everything, from pamphlets to starter kits, and to your entire product range.

If you make a promise – keep it

Just about the most demotivating experience in network marketing is to have your upline promise something but not deliver it. If your downlines come to perceive you as being all talk and no action they will cease to listen to anything you say. Need I say more? In this business integrity rules.

Use record cards

Each person you bring into the business should be allotted either a file or a record card, or both. Keep notes of what they have achieved, their hobbies, birthday, spouse's name and birthday, children's names and birthdays, etc.

In a similiar way to breaking promises, an upline who forgets what is, to you, important aspects of your life − or, worse, confuses you with someone else − is not going to endear themselves to you. Quite often the small things in life can make or break a relationship. Whether we are talking about a relationship of marriage or business makes little difference.

The remembering of a birthday; a promise kept; the remembering of some aspect of your downline's life which has importance to them. These actions can speak louder than thousands of eloquent words. Enter important details into your associate's file record − don't think you can keep it all in your head − and refer to it when the time comes to talk with that person again. Such consideration will pay dividends. Try it.

Reviving the dropouts

Make sure you find ways to stay in touch with those who drop out as it is common for someone who appeared dead to be rekindled into life. You could contact them in the following ways:

- You could send them cards at Christmas and for their birthday.
- You could send 'wish you were here' cards from your holiday destinations or from the exotic hotel where you are staying during your company-paid-for seminar.
- You could send them testimonial letters to the effectiveness of your business plan, and announcements of new product lines.
- When you know of an especially good meeting coming up locally − perhaps with a motivating and successful guest speaker − send them an invitation.

Use your imagination and find original ways to maintain contact. The New Year can be a good time, when everybody is short of money after Christmas; also after the school and annual holidays in early September.

You may find that some people will wait to see how you make out before making a commitment themselves. For others the timing may not have been appropriate the first time you spoke and your renewed contact may be welcomed.

Your people will do what you do

It is well known that the general who leads from the front will command the respect of his troops. This principle applies as much to business as it does to the field of battle. The example you set will be copied by your downlines, which will be copied by their downlines, and so on, and so on. You get the picture.

A common factor running through all firms is that the morale of the work-force is intimately linked to the attitude of the top-level management. If you want people to work hard you must treat them as you would expect to be treated, and do as you are asking them to do. Anything less and you soon lose their respect and co-operation. In every aspect of your business you must set the highest of examples.

Be honest

The 'fake it 'til you make it' approach advocated by some of the more dubious companies is where you buy the expensive car and the flash suits before your income can actually justify it.

This approach is common in traditional industries where there are valuable clients to impress and lucrative contracts at stake. Its value in network marketing is doubtful, however. The straightforward admission that you have only recently started in the business, and therefore have not yet had the time to amass great wealth, is readily accepted by the majority of people.

In the long run, rather than adopting some glitzy, second-hand-car-salesman-made-good act, you will make a better impression on your friends and prospects, will be happier and will have considerably more peace of mind if you tell the simple truth. If you offer a good service to your customers and downlines, and combine this with persistent effort, you will generate an aura of relaxed confidence that will inspire trust and credibility.

Give others respect

I have noticed that some people in sales seem to consider their fellow human beings as nothing but instruments to further their own acquisition of wealth. They have no respect for the sanctity of their customers' individual space.

If you want others to respect you (and who is going to want to emulate someone they do not respect?), then you must first give your fellow men and women the respect they deserve as thinking, feeling individuals.

Listen to what others are saying

There are two types of people in life: those who listen, and those who hear. Most people can hear, but listening is more of an art. If you listen to your upline, you will learn. If you listen to your downlines, you will be able to identify their problems, and thus help solve them before they quit the business in frustration. And if you listen to your customer's objections to buying, and answer them, you will increase your sales dramatically.

SUCCESS CHECK

How to treat your customers and downlines:

★ be honest

★ respect them

★ listen to what they have to say

Like attracts like

Quality attracts quality. Have you noticed how people of like mind seem to congregate together? The same is as true in business as it is in the pub or social club. If you want to attract people who are hard working, enthusiastic, ethical and honest into your business, you must first develop these qualities yourself.

With consistent efforts over a period of time you will become like a magnet, attracting people of similar ideals to yourself into your business.

SUCCESS CHECK

★ Develop in yourself the qualities you want to see in your downlines

---

If in doubt, return to basics

If you run into difficulties, don't go off looking for some new, magic answer to your problem. Simply return to the basics of the business: recruit, sponsor, communicate, go to meetings, etc.

This is a simple business. If it is worked correctly and consistently, the rewards will come naturally. Nine times out of ten, when people develop problems it is because they are complicating things.

If you are the one with a problem look for the simple solutions. Remember to KISS. This translates as 'keep it simple and straightforward', or 'keep it simple — stupid'! I prefer the latter as it really sticks in your mind!

SUCCESS CHECK

★ KEEP YOUR BUSINESS SIMPLE

Accomplishing small goals brings you closer to your big goals

In 1963 John F Kennedy gave the USA the goal of landing a man on the moon by the end of that decade. How was such an awesome target achieved?

What NASA (National Aeronautical and Space Administration) did was to break the big, distant goal — landing on the moon — down into a series of smaller, more easily attainable goals. They built the small, one-man Mercury craft. Then they moved on to the two-man Gemini missions. Finally, they created the three-man Apollo capsules which would eventually take man to the moon.

148

NASA's persistent effort and consistent work to overcome one problem at a time — setting themselves one small goal after another, and achieving them — eventually led to the accomplishment of their big goal and those immortal words, 'That is one small step for a man ...'

Network Marketing Success Story
BRIAN and BARBARA JACQUES
Leighton Buzzard, Bedfordshire

One way or another, Brian and Barbara Jacques have been involved in direct sales for over twenty years. They chose Nature's Sunshine because it is an ethical, family-based company which has been well established internationally since 1972. They saw it is a company which has shown steady growth over a number of years and they felt this gave a good indication of the degree of security they would enjoy.

Brian and Barbara like network marketing because the business costs next to nothing to start and, if you are good at it, you can generate a fantastic income within a relatively short space of time. Nature's Sunshine is the only network marketing company they work with, feeling that it would be difficult to do justice to more than one product range at a time, due to the split commitment inherent in multiple operations.

They do, however, run a colour and image analysis consultancy and training business. Barbara has even written a book on the subject. They find that this blends well with Nature's Sunshine, since a large part of looking good is feeling good — and one of the best ways to feel good is to feed your body the correct nutrients. So, the two independent businesses harmonise without conflict, often, in fact, building themselves synergistically.

All Brian and Barbara's customers buy at wholesale prices, as they sign everyone into their business. This approach has several benefits:

- the customers get their products at a reduced price from the normal retail price;
- everyone is presented with the opportunity to sponsor others and become involved in network marketing;

149

- the chances of customers becoming active downlines increases over the percentage who would do this if they were purely retail customers. Therefore, Brian and Barbara's profits increase.

In the early days of their business they set up a national network very quickly, but the costs of maintaining it (travel, telephone, etc) were very high. With hindsight they would now stay closer to home until they had created a business with strong foundations.

They stress that you should not expect to make a huge amount out of the business straight away, as a network takes time to build. For this reason they prefer to sponsor both husband and wife so that both know the reasons why relatively little immediate money comes in. If both partners do not realise that the rewards come after a period of sustained effort, there will often be problems. Brian and Barbara teach everyone to take the long-term view. They teach patience: you can create a substantial income – but it is going to take time, energy and commitment.

14. YOUR FUTURE IN NETWORK MARKETING

$\mathbf{Y}$OU will find that some people, when you tell them about your new business, will try to laugh away your dream. Don't let them. People who indulge in ridicule are usually ignorant and frightened. Too frightened to do anything themselves, they try to destroy the hopes of others.

But people like this can only hurt you if you let them, if you let their negativity get inside you. Keep them out; after all, you wouldn't allow someone to wreck your living room, would you? So don't allow them to wreck your dreams. You must learn to be indifferent to these people and to shut them out of your life. Associate only with positive, successful people and you will find some of their magic rubbing off on you.

Set your goals and beat them. Then set more. The attitude of making life work for you, as opposed to working to live, will be the successful attitude.

Put first things first

The world is littered with successful business people who have created great wealth, only to lose their spouse and families in the divorce courts. Success means an awful lot more than the mere accumulation of money. It means living a balanced life, sharing with your loved ones the benefits your business has brought you; and it means creating time for yourself and for your leisure activities.

Be flexible when you are developing that delicate harmony between your business, social, family and spiritual lives. Aim to be a success in all aspects of your life, not just one or two. Be proud of your achievements. They may not be the same as someone else's, but they are yours.

Value time as a precious commodity. Work hard at your business; that is admirable. But don't neglect your family. Your children (if you have them) will only be young once and − although they can be frustrating at times − wouldn't it be sad to look back in twenty years only to realise you had missed out on them growing up?

Discover what motivates you

To keep going in network marketing you need to have developed a strong sense of purpose. The simple earning of money is often not sufficient a reason for many people to make a strong commitment. You need to develop a powerful purpose, a reason for action − a dream. And you need to encourage and teach your downlines to do likewise.

Success means different things to different people. For some, success means power. Many see it as security. For still others it may mean the material trappings of wealth − the big car, the luxury home or the lavish lifestyle. And don't overlook the more esoteric reasons such as peace of mind, or the capacity to spend more time in social or religious voluntary work.

You will come across some rich people who are unhappy, but you also will come upon poor people who are unhappy. The opposite is also true. Unhappiness is not created by money, only an undue attachment to it. I believe that, in general, most people are happier when they have a high income. It takes the pressure off paying the bills, and most of us can handle the rest of life's problems much more easily when we are not stressed by monetary worries.

True success comes from within. It has to do with your personal self-satisfaction, and with how good you feel about yourself. From time to time you will run into problems with some of the people in your business. It is an interesting fact that we all feel better about ourselves, and get more done, when we practise increasing self-control, patience and compassion for those less able than ourselves.

The future starts here

There is the story of the motorist who was lost and who stopped to ask the way of a farmer leaning on a farm gate. 'Well', said the farmer, 'it's easy to get to the place you're looking for, but this isn't the best place to start from!'

That may be a crazy story, but it's the way so many people think. They say, 'I'll start my business after I've done this', or, 'I need to be in the right mood to get going. I'll really try to do something tomorrow.' Of course, there is always something else which needs doing; and tomorrow never comes.

Change comes only from action. The best time you will ever have to start your business is *today*. If you start building your network in the now of today, it will be bringing you gold nuggets in the now of the future.

Work your way through this book several times. Keep studying. No one ever reaches the point of knowing everything about any subject and you will find more hidden in these pages after a few months' experience in the business than you did when you were a novice.

Finally, remember that, with determination and persistence, you *can* make your dreams come true.

GLOSSARY: Network Marketing Terminology

Direct distributors: People who have reached a certain level of sales volume. Once that point is reached they order further product direct from the company instead of via their upline.

Direct selling: The distribution of goods direct from manufacturer to consumer, without wholesale or retail intermediaries.

Distributors: The people who sell the products. Also called associates, dealers, representatives, consultants and agents.

Downline: Someone you introduce to, and sign into, your business. You are your downline's upline.

Frontline: People sponsored directly by you.

Group volume: A distributor's personal volume and that of their downlines.

Levels: Likened to generations within your own family. You are your own first level, the person you sponsor is your second, the person they sponsor is your third, the person they introduce is your fourth level, and the person they sponsor is your fifth. Hence the term multi-level marketing.

MLM: Multi-level marketing.

Network marketing: Used interchangeably with multi-level marketing, it describes the network of dealers that a successful distributor sets up around the country.

Presentation: The act of showing the product or business to a prospect.

Prospect: Someone you are considering as a potential purchaser of your product, or as a recruit to your business.

Retail profit: The difference between the price paid by you to the company — the wholesale price — and the price you charge your customer.

Sponsoring: The act of introducing new people into your business as distributors.

Upline: The person who introduces you to, and signs you with, your parent company, and who is primarily responsible for your training and for providing you with information concerning your business.

APPENDIX A: The Direct Selling Association (DSA)

FORMED in 1965, the DSA is the trade association of the direct selling industry. It accounts for 75 per cent of all direct sales and 60 per cent of all registered direct selling companies. Its objectives are to bring together the ethical companies involved in direct selling and to promote the highest standards of trading practice and consumer protection.

Companies are subject to detailed vetting before being admitted to the association. This ensures that standards remain high. All member companies must adhere to the DSA's code of practice, which was drawn up in close consultation with the Office of Fair Trading. This code provides as follows.

(a) All sales people should clearly indentify their company and the products they sell, and act with integrity during their sales presentations.

(b) Customers should be offered a fourteen-day cooling-off period during which any order may be cancelled and any deposit refunded.

(c) Member companies must comply with the judgement of the DSA's independent code administrator with respect to any consumer complaint.

Full details of the DSA, and a list of member companies, can be obtained by writing to: Direct Selling Association, 44 Russell Square, London, WC1B 4JP. Tel: 071 580 8433.

APPENDIX B: The Fair Trading Regulations

IN Chapter 1 of this book the myth that network marketing, or multi-level marketing, is the same as those notorious pyradmid-selling schemes which abounded in the 1960s and 1970s was hopefully dispelled. There is also a technical point which should also be considered.

In 1973 the Office of Fair Trading Pyramid Selling Schemes Act became law and was revised by the Pyramid Selling Schemes Regulations 1989 and 1990. These regulations effectively outlawed the unscrupulous garage-filling schemes (explained earlier) in which many people lost a lot of money. This was all to the good. Unfortunately, it also forces legitimate network marketing companies to operate under the technical heading of pyramid selling!

This is obviously misleading and the DSA has lobbied the Department of Trade and Industry to change the name of these regulations, since they put perfectly reputable companies into the same bed as the criminals. At the time of writing, however, this anomaly of the law is still current.

So, if you should run into someone who puts forward the argument that, as the government sees fit to lump network marketing in with pyramid selling, that in fact must be the case – you can simply inform them that it is merely a technicality.

If you would like to read the regulations – and it is well worth knowing the law as it applies to any business – copies may be obtained from the DSA. See Appendix A for their address.

USEFUL INFORMATION

Books

Hill, Napoleon, *Think and Grow Rich* (Wilshire Book Company, 12015 Sherman Road, Hollywood, California 91605, USA).

— and Stone, W Clement, *Success Through a Positive Mental Attitude* (Thorsons).

Jonson MD, Spencer and Wilson, Larry, *The One-Minute Sales Person* (Fontana).

Kennedy, Gavin, *Everything is Negotiable* (Arrow Books).

Leeds, Dorothy, *Powerspeak* (Piatkus Books).

Ley, D Forbes, *The Best Seller* (Kogan Page).

Twitchell, Paul, *The Flute of God* (ECKANKAR, Attn: ECK Materials, PO Box 27300, Minneapolis MN55427, USA. Credit cards: Tel: 612 544 0066).

Wattles, Wallace D, *Financial Success Through Creative Thought (The Science of Getting Rich)* (The Metaphiscal Research Group, Archers Court, Stonestyle Lane, Hastings, England, TN35 4PG. Or, Health Research, Box 70, Mokelumne Hill, California, USA).

Tapes

Waitley, Dennis, *The Psychology of Winning*. Available from Nightingale-Conant Corporation, Unit 10, Mitcham Industrial Estate, Streatham Rd, Mitcham, Surrey, CR4 2AP.

Shepherd, Roy, *Yes You Can*. Available from The Celebrity Store, PO Box 150, Twickenham, TW1 3RF.

Courses

The Life Training, 16 Talbot Road, London W2. For further information on a wide range of self-awareness training courses, tel: 071-727 0652.

158

INDEX

Business Books for Successful Managers

PIATKUS BUSINESS BOOKS have been created for people like you, busy executives and managers who need expert knowledge readily available in clear and easy-to-follow format. All the books are written by specialists in their field. They will help you improve your skills quickly and effortlessly in the workplace and on a personal level.

Each book is packed with ideas and good advice which can be put into practice immediately. Titles include:

The Art of the Hard Sell *Subtle high pressure tactics that really work* Robert L. Shook

The Best Person for the Job *Where to find them and how to keep them* Malcolm Bird

Beware the Naked Man Who Offers You His Shirt *Do what you love, love what you do and deliver more than you promise* Harvey Mackay

Brain Power *The 12-week mental training programme* Marilyn vos Savant and Leonore Fleischer

The Complete Book of Business Etiquette Lynne Brennan and David Block

Confident Decision Making *How to make the right decision every time* J. Edward Russo and Paul J. H. Schoemaker

The Complete Time Management System Christian H. Godefroy

Dealing with Difficult People *How to improve your communication skills in the workplace* Roberta Cava

The Energy Factor *How to motivate your workforce* Art McNeil

How to Become Rich and Successful *A 14-point plan for Business Success* Charles Templeton

How to Close Every Sale Joe Girard with Robert L. Shook

How to Collect the Money You Are Owed *Improve your cash flow and increase your profit* Malcolm Bird

How to Develop and Profit from Your Creative Powers *Simple techniques for creating new ideas* Michael LeBoeuf

How to Succeed in Network Marketing Leonard Hawkins

How to Win Customers and Keep Them for Life   Michael LeBoeuf

Improve Your Profits *Practical advice for the small- to medium-sized business*   Malcolm Bird

The Influential Woman *How to achieve success without losing your femininity*   Lee Bryce

Leadership Skills for Every Manager *New techniques to improve organisational effectiveness*   Jim Clemmer and Art McNeil

Mentoring and Networking *A woman's guide*   Dr Lily Segerman-Peck

Marketing Yourself *How to sell yourself and get the jobs you've always wanted*   Dorothy Leeds

Organise Yourself   Ronni Eisenberg with Kate Kelly

Powerspeak *The complete guide to public speaking and communication* Dorothy Leeds

The PowerTalk System *How to communicate effectively* Christian H. Godefroy and Stephanie Barrat

Selling by Direct Mail *An entrepreneurial guide to direct marketing* John W. Graham and Susan K. Jones

Status *What it is and how to achieve it*   Philippa Davies

The Strategy of Meetings   George David Kieffer

Telephone Selling Techniques that Really Work *How to find new business by phone*   Bill Good

Your Memory *How it works and how to improve it*   Kenneth L. Higbee

Your Total Image *How to communicate success*   Philippa Davies

You too can benefit from expert advice. Just look out for our distinctive Piatkus silver business book jackets in the shops. For a free brochure with further information on our complete range of business titles, please write to:

Business Books Department
Piatkus Books
5 Windmill Street
London, W1P 1HF

PIATKUS